MW00681232

COOKIES DO
CRUMBLE

DR. CLAUDIA WELLS-HAMILTON

An Autobiography

COOKIES DO
CRUMBLE

TATE PUBLISHING
AND ENTERPRISES, LLC

Cookies Do Crumble

Copyright © 2013 by Dr. Claudia Wells-Hamilton. All rights reserved.

No part of this publication may be reproduced, stored in a retrieval system or transmitted in any way by any means, electronic, mechanical, photocopy, recording or otherwise without the prior permission of the author except as provided by USA copyright law.

The opinions expressed by the author are not necessarily those of Tate Publishing, LLC.

Published by Tate Publishing & Enterprises, LLC
127 E. Trade Center Terrace | Mustang, Oklahoma 73064 USA
1.888.361.9473 | www.tatepublishing.com

Tate Publishing is committed to excellence in the publishing industry. The company reflects the philosophy established by the founders, based on Psalm 68:11,
"The Lord gave the word and great was the company of those who published it."

Book design copyright © 2013 by Tate Publishing, LLC. All rights reserved.
Cover design by Rtor Maghuyop
Interior design by Mary Jean Archival

Published in the United States of America

ISBN: 978-1-62902-116-4
1. BIOGRAPHY & AUTOBIOGRAPHY / Personal Memoirs
2. BIOGRAPHY & AUTOBIOGRAPHY / Educators
13.09.16

DEDICATION

This book is dedicated to my beloved natural and spiritual families who have encouraged and supported me as I entered the chapters of growth, changes and adjustments. Because of my families, I have been able to view life with a keen, sensitive eye.

There have been numerous victories, accomplishments, academic degrees, promotions and accolades. Someone was always in the wings cheering me on, and inspiring me to do a little more and to ascend to my highest denominator. God has never left me without support.

Then, there were the sad times, the bereavements, the illnesses and more disappointments, inherent with life. During these times, there was always someone reminding me that I was strong and capable of exercising an abundance of faith. My natural and spiritual families, along with friends, could always be counted on to supply the tissues, flowers or cards to encourage me. I had company when I laughed; company when I cried. God has never left me without the support of my natural or spiritual families.

ACKNOWLEDGEMENTS

Bishop Wyoming Wells, my late beloved father and role model

Edmond Scott Hamilton, my devoted, loving husband who has always supported me

Mary E. Wells, my precious late mother, who enabled me and stood strong by me

Thaddeus Raydell Hunt, my son, who challenges me and brings flowers and gifts

Jason Thaddeus Hunt, grandson, who taught me patience and lovingly kept my secrets

Emma Johanna Addison Hunt, my granddaughter, who came from Sweden to be near

DeOla Wells Johnson, my sister, who always listens and prays for and with me

Gayle and Toney Mooney, loving, thoughtful niece and nephew who are there for me

Kathryn Hamilton Rogers, daughter, who dressed my wounds and showed me love

Inez and Laddie P. Bell*, loyal, lifelong friends

Wilda Elizabeth Newton, my late covenant sister, who drove miles to help

Georgia Pearl Hill, covenant sister, who bathed my unpleasant wounds

Rose Malenfant, neighbor, who took me to chemotherapy

Virginia Love, M.D., my late psychiatrist friend, who professionally advised me

Lisa Wynette Murphy, M.D., "niece", who sat, listened, and gave medical advice

Willie Mae Gordon Sheard, a true, spiritual sister who comforted and stood by me

Mabel Corey Higgs, a supportive friend and spiritual sister who is always there for me

Teresa Regina Lenon, my surrogate daughter who keeps in touch

Barbara Davis Benford, a constant friend, who has always been there for me

Annis Lucille Dunlap, made the healing oxtail soup that restored my appetite

Bishop Clifford Dunlap, my late pastor and kind shepherd who watched for my soul

The praying Church of God in Christ Saints, in Detroit, Flint, Greensboro and Memphis

SPECIAL ACKNOWLEDGEMENT

Prophetess Stephanie Moore, to whom I owe the completion of this book

CONTENTS

FOREWORD

One's self perception is vital in determining one's behavior. A cookie is a cake made from stiff dough. No matter how crusty or hard the dough is on the outside, it is always sweet inside.

I perceive myself to be the human replica of a cookie. I am independent, candid, opinionated and "take charge" on the outside, but generous, kind, dependable, loyal, friendly and compassionate on the inside. Thus, my life has been lived in a fashion that reflects my self-perception as a cookie.

Even though the dough of a cookie is soft, it has to be rolled, shaped, sliced and baked to a hard consistency. Notwithstanding, the hardness, there are pressures that can make the cookie crumble. Nevertheless, I want to be a tough cookie.

INTRODUCTION

I stood there holding my husband's hand. The news stunned me, even though I was fully aware of the pros and cons of the situation in which I had found myself. There was nothing left to say. I was going to die. I felt that I was facing an inevitable death, and I stood silently and humbly before God and His mercy. I must hold my head up high and be somebody, even when facing death.

HERE SHE COMES

It was January 17, 1930, a cold morning in Philadelphia, Pennsylvania. It would have been a typical day if the young newlywed had not begun having severe pains in her belly.

Mary Wells, a young wife, was temporarily in her mother's home to have support when she gave birth to her first baby. Wyoming, the young minister who she had married a year or so ago, was ninety miles away in Mt. Union, Pennsylvania, where he had been appointed the pastor of a church.

It was time to see the world, so the baby could not wait for the father, and made her scheduled arrival into the world, just as the rays of the morning sun appeared in the east.

It was a seven pound girl.

Young and excited, she did not wait to consult her husband, and Mary named the baby "Viola".

The proud father arrived in Philadelphia the next day.

He rushed into the hospital to go to the nursery first to see his firstborn. Like most men, he had hoped for a boy, but it was okay that the baby was a girl.

Mary was so happy and relieved when her husband joined her in her hospital room.

"Did you see the baby?" she asked.

Smiling and brimming with pride, his response was, "Yes, and she is beautiful with a head full of hair. She sorta looks like both of us."

"Yes. She is beautiful." There was a brief pause before Mary said, "I have already named her Viola."

"Viola!" he shouted emphatically." I don't want her named Viola. That is the name of that drunk woman down the street from us. We must change her name immediately."

So it was agreed on that the new member of the family would be renamed Claudia Wyona.

As soon as he could, Wyoming left Philadelphia and drove his wife and daughter in his new Chevrolet to their home in Mt. Union, Pennsylvania.

HOME, SWEET HOME

Mt. Union, Pennsylvania, was a small town where the main industry was making bricks. It was nestled in a valley on the banks of a subsidiary river of the Susquehanna River surrounded by the Allegheny Mountains.

Times were not very good in 1930. A depression gripped the United States. Men had to stand in soup lines or had to work in government C.C. Camps to provide minimal needs for their families. In desperation, home invasions were committed to find food and to eat anything available in the invaded home.

Being in the ministry, allowed Elder Wells some promise of an income, be it as small as a nickel, an amount that he received in one of his weekly free will offerings. To subsidize his offerings, a Pound List was read.

A Pound List is a grocery list that was read at the end of the Friday prayer meeting service. The members were asked to volunteer to bring a pound of a food item to the pastor's house on Saturday.

"Who'll give some potatoes?" Sister Martin would ask.

"I will." A parishioner would respond, and so the name would go beside potatoes.

After the items on the Pound List were promised, Sister Martin would give Mother the list for her reference on the next day, Saturday.

Thus, food was put in the pastor's pantry. It was sparse, but ample. It helped to avoid the soup line and to feed his growing family of a wife and three, small children.

A fight for survival began in infancy. I became susceptible to pneumonia and every childhood communicable disease in the area, including Scarlet Fever. Many days were spent in the local hospital or thirty days in a house with a Quarantine sign on the door. If I were to survive, I would have to fight for my life.

Elder Wells was warned by the health department that due to the house quarantine, he could not stay in the house and preach in his pulpit. So a cat and mouse game ensued with his slipping in the house at night and out early in the morning to stay across the street with a parishioner. It took two adults to care for this growing family with a sickly child and two toddlers, and he did what he felt that he had to do.

"Mama," the name the doctor affectionately called the young mother, Mary, "you are going to have to fight for this baby's life."

So she did, with the help of her husband, special prayers, the church members and her mother-in-law, Mother Louisa Wells, who would ride the train to Mt. Union for hours to mix herbs taken from the back yard and to apply them on her my chest as poultice.

I, nevertheless, evolved from continuous episodes of poor health to a rather sturdy, robust toddler. The high fevers had not affected my brains, and I developed an extreme inquisitive nature. I often asked, "Why?", when asking a question was forbidden because it indicated rebellion. The questioning of adults was not tolerated, under any circumstances.

The adults who observed this inquisitive nature warned the young mother that her child was too grown, an expression that meant that her behavior was unacceptable. Somehow, even though the parents somewhat shared the same opinion, when alone at home, not under the scrutiny of others, they chose to pretend not to notice the "Why?" and the "Why not?" It was an unspoken double standard, that silence was preferred to be observed by their daughter in the presence of the parents' peers.

Six was rather a young age to develop strategy, but it seems that a strategy for peaceful survival was being practiced. It was necessary to learn when to speak and when not to speak. On one occasion, a church missionary, a friend of my mother's was harsh in her criticism of me and made a negative prediction of my future. Interestingly enough, much later in my early adult age, her daughter became an alcoholic and I became a professional. The missionary saw me at a convention, complimented me, and asked me to buy her a purse like the one that I was using. I would have bought her one, but the past hurt was too deep to oblige her. Words can hurt like sticks and stones; don't let anyone fool you.

On the other hand, there are very fond memories of ministers, Elder Calvin Williams and Bishop Dewitt Arthur Burton, my father's colleagues. When intervention was needed, my parents were persuaded to give me a nickel to attend my one, and only puppet show and to receive my first two wheeled bicycle. These two ministers observed my personality, but did not criticize my proclivity to be a bit mature for my chronological age.

It was 1936. It had been raining for days, and I overheard Daddy telling my Mother that he was going back down with some of the neighbors to see how much the river had risen. There was talk that the nearby Juniata River was rising rapidly. The heavy rain had precluded our playing outside, and for some reason, unknown to me, mother did not send me to school.

Then, it happened late over in the night right after bedtime. There was a very loud knock on our front door. Brother Knox was frantically saying, "Elder Wells, Elder Wells, get your family out! The dam has busted."

What was a dam and what made it" bust" and cause the water to come up on our street? Wasn't dam a curse word? I could not comprehend what was going on, but I knew that, based on my parents' bustling, we had to get out in a hurry.

"Claudia, grab some clothes, and come on." My mother frantically called out as she grabbed her baby girl and proceeded to the stairs. "Hurry!" she ordered as she grabbed some blankets and some coats. Our sister, Eva, was suffering from St Findus Dance and seemed oblivious to the situation as she was carried to the waiting car wrapped in a brown blanket.

I grabbed a few dirty clothes out of the clothes hamper as I scampered down the stairs to get in the waiting car, and we were taken to a parishioner's home on higher ground.

We lived in a part of the town a little distance from the mountain that was called, The Flats. There were about a hundred people living in The Flats, all of whom had joined in the evacuation.

Early on the next morning my father, this six foot two lean, man, my mother and I, went to the railroad track to observe the damage being caused by the flood. My father cried. There were also quiet sobs by others and looks of despair. The mood was somber; fear could be sensed.

A few of the women were also crying and singing. It was so eerie. I had never seen my father cry before. Seeing him cry saddened and frightened me, making me aware of the possibility that maybe we were not safe. Was the water going to come up to the railroad track or was the train going to come and hit us?

"Elder Wells, everything is gonna be alright." Someone in crowd said in an attempt to comfort him.

We stood helplessly and watched furniture, live stock and personal belongings float down the street. A neighboring house across the street from our house was swept off of its foundation, turned at a right angle and it hit the church that my father was pastoring. Not being able to withstand the impact, the church building swayed and moved half way off of its foundation. This caused pandemonium among us.

A deep feeling of desperation, not fully understood by a six year old, came over me. Our house was halfway under water. The street, where a few days ago I had placed my hopscotch numbers, was no longer there. We recognized some of our furniture and items floating slowly down the street. I began to wonder what were we going to do because it appeared that all of our possessions were being washed away down the street. Even though only six years old, it became apparent to me that as the oldest, that I must appear to be a big girl, and that I could not cry, even though my prized colored doll baby that my grandmother had given me for Christmas was possibly washed away down Walnut Street.

My grandmother had paid the enormous sum of $5.00 for the doll, and the saints had come by our house just to see this expensive colored doll.

Somehow, some details escape me. We escaped harm, but we were left homeless. Fortunately, the church mother, a senior citizen, had opened her doors to us. It was very difficult to abide by her preference that the children not allowed to play in the house. My brother's running a toy truck on the linoleum floor brought a stern reprimand. It was an uncomfortable situation, but there were no alternatives. We wore Red Cross clothes, ate lots of white potato soup, slept on the floor and tried to stay as quiet as possible. We had nothing but an open door. We were told by our parents to be thankful, and I was, but it seemed like we stayed forever at that house.

Those unpleasant memories were balanced by recalling the day when a month or two later, we ceremoniously marched singing down the street, with our new clothes on, to our renovated church. The Pentecostal charismatic congregation shouted and gave God plenty of praises. I shouted, too. I was finally relieved.

Returning to our home, however, was challenging. Mud was thick everywhere. The moldy smell penetrated everything. I remembered trying to retrieve my school books that were covered with mud. Everything had to be boiled and bleached before using. Imagine shoveling mud out of your house and scraping mud off of the furniture that was left. My only previous experience with mud had been mud cakes and there was enough mud for hundreds of hoecakes.

THE SHAPING

Being young, I was naturally very flexible, and ready to take on a definite shape by the master bakers, my parents. They realized this early on and began instilling moral codes and practices. They controlled the *oven* and they knew that they were going to make it hot, or some might prefer to call it strict.

My parents noticed my outgoing personality and friendliness, both as an asset and as a liability. Regardless of the resistance, they were determined to shape me to be likeable and strong. They first began working on my personality.

Ministers and their families were highly respected in the small Pennsylvania community. My parents, especially my father, insisted that I did not develop into a bragging, haughty, conceited brat. On the other hand, my mother preached daily to, "Hold your head up high and be somebody." Those were her precise words. So, it was assumed that it was expected of me to balance both humility and pride.

The young girls from the church were invited and welcomed into our home. I had to share my toys and include them in my games. It was very rare for my mother to permit me to visit any of the girls in their homes.

One unsupervised visit to a neighbor's home exposed me to an unusual game. A teenager, a visiting niece of one of the deacons and his wife, devised a new game for us to play one rainy day when she grew weary of playing, My car, Your car. My car, Your car was a game where we would take alternate ownership of passing cars to see who would get the most pretty cars. Early during the game, this visiting niece suggested that we leave the front porch and go into the kitchen, lie on the floor and take our panties off. Never having played this game, I proceeded to remove my underpants. She attempted to get on top of me. I had no idea what was to come next, but I told her that I did not like that game and put my underpants back on. I did not know the name and the rules of this game. I just did not want to play the game with the girl on top of me. No offense meant. It was just not my choice for fun. I liked playing, My car, Your car better.

There was little needed to encourage friendliness to the young boys. My proclivity ran in that direction. I was very clumsy, but clumsiness did not preclude involvement in the daily games, especially Hide and Go Seek. My hiding was under constant observation by my parents or my sister, Eva, who reported to mother frequently.

"Mama, Claudia is hiding in the garage."

I was sought and found by my vigilant mother before being found by the seekers.

Years later, being inquisitive became a desired activity, and I began to seek knowledge. Reading became an obsession, and I read every chance that I got. It was obvious that household chores did not have the fascination that a book had. In fact, I avoided every household chore to the extent that I was frequently referred to as being lazy. Often, I would go between the bed and the wall with a small light to read when I was expected to be setting the table for dinner. Ayn Rand's, *The Fountainhead*, was one of my favorites. In later years, I stayed up all night and read her *Atlas Shrugged. Little Women*, by Louisa Mae Alcott did not capture my full attention. I enjoyed more mature books.

Early on, integrity and honesty had to be instilled during my shaping.

Sunday School books were available in an abundance in our home since they were distributed to the Sunday school officials by my father. Once, I got my hands on some expired Sunday School books and saw this as an opportunity to make some money. I persuaded my young brother to assist me in going around the neighborhood to sell the expired Sunday School books for a penny. When my father became aware of this, the rod came out and an order was sternly given that I return the pennies. Subsequently, I made up the story that I had mistakenly sold them the wrong issue and was returning their money. Thus, a little dignity was reserved for my brother and me in the neighborhood, but it was not too pleasant for a day or two at home. Thus, ended my attempt as an entrepreneur.

Honesty and integrity had to be reinforced. Several attempts had to be made, on my behalf, on my parents' part. My vices were petty food thefts. Stealing butter to lick on and over tasting the bread pudding placed in the ice box to cool for after church dessert. The lesson not to steal bread pudding was instilled so successfully by my vomiting and the rod, until I have not eaten bread pudding since I was seven years old.

The rod does work effectively, sometimes for a lifetime. My parents, especially my mother, believed and practiced corporal punishment. In fact if corporal punishment had been illegal when I was a child, my mother would have been given a stiff jail sentence and would possibly have been a lifetime parolee.

We moved from Mt. Union, Pennsylvania to Harrisburg, Pennsylvania, when I was eight years old, because my father had been reassigned to pastor Broad Street Church of God in Christ, a Pentecostal holiness church. The people who attended the Pentecostal holiness church were called the Saints. Pentecostal holiness members were ridiculed because of their charismatic services. The shouting, tambourine beating, and guitar playing were amusing to non-members. So not only did I catch the wrath of my peers for being the teacher's pet, I was further personally ridicule for being a Holy Roller, the nickname used to refer to us. It was reputed that when we were rejoicing that we would fall and roll on the floor sometimes in sawdust.

The Saints encouraged me to excel in my studies, and whenever the school had an open house, my mother and the Saints would go to the school to see my work on exhibit. My nickname until I was eight years old was, Pluckum, and the Saints, some who really did not know my christened name, would ask to see Pluckum's work. Paragraphs written by me would be displayed all around the room, along with my handwriting exercises.

It was also at this time in Harrisburg that Mother would give me my monthly quarter so that I could go to hear the Harrisburg Symphony Orchestra. My appreciation for classical music like *Peer Gynt Suite* was developed. My initial reason for wanting to go was to show off, because only few classmates' parents could afford to give them a quarter. I also got a chance to get rid of my braids for Shirley Temple curls and to wear one of my Sunday, special, dresses. It did not take long, however, before that attitude changed, and I looked forward to appreciating the different instruments and identifying movements of the musical scores. I developed a lifelong appreciation for classical music.

On several occasions, Daddy would brag to his friend about how smart I was. I would overhear him. In reflection, I believe that he intended for me to hear him as an incentive. Nothing was more pleasing than to hear him say, "D.A., that Claudia is as smart as a whip." So it became my goal to be the smartest girl in every aspect of my life.

My social studies teacher at Hamilton Street Elementary School had round robin reading. It did not take long to realize that she would let you read until you made a mistake. When she called on me to read, I tried to read for the entire time left for reading. To enhance it, I would read with expression and syllabicate difficult words. She would be delighted, and would express her delight to the class. This did not set too well with them, and when she left me in charge of the class to record names of misbehaviors while she was out of the room. I made enemies out of the bullies. You see, this was a test of my reliability, as often she would be outside peeping in observing the misbehavior. I had to report the infractions of the teacher's rules. Maybe this could be considered being between a rock and a hard place.

When I finally went outside to go home, a crowd would be waiting saying, "Here she comes!" Even though I lived diagonally across the street from the school, I could not make it home. One bully in particular, took delight in beating me until I fell to the ground. What a price to pay for being the teacher's pet or favorite. Maybe, it was time for me learn to defend myself. My mother and my Sunday School teacher had told me not to fight. I was to turn my cheeks. So, I had rotating bruised cheeks.

Mother, after frequently seeing me come home bruised and crying, changed the order from, "Don't fight." to "You better stop letting them beat you up!" This gave me little bolster because the girls who beat me were strong and from families of parents who drank a lot. These people were labeled *bad*, and all of their sisters and cousins would jump in, if necessary. I was no match for them, so I was still intimidated.

Soon after the order had changed for me to defend myself, the bad girls got bored with beating me up and ignored me. One male classmate, Joseph Range, decided that he would try his hand at beating me after I had turned his name in for talking while the teacher was out. Everyone was shocked when I closed my eyes, turned on Joseph with flailing fists and beat him into a surrender. The crowd went wild. I could not believe what I had accomplished, I had finally emerged as a winner. The humiliation for Joseph was so great until he, eventually, became friendly to me for solace. Joseph became my first boyfriend.

Afterwards, in class during devotions, when I was allowed to select a song to sing, I would select, "Home on the Range" to express my deep love for Joseph.

Three years later, in 1941, another geographical change in my life. My father received a clergy promotion that necessitated our moving from Harrisburg, Pennsylvania to Greensboro, North Carolina. My teachers questioned why my parents would move their bright children from a northern to a southern school system. It had to happen because our church founder, Bishop Charles H. Mason, had promoted my father to an Overseer with almost one-hundred churches in his diocese. At first, he had appointed my father to go to Minnesota, but he immediately had second thoughts and said that, "It will be too cold for the little children." Bishop Mason changed his mind, and Daddy was appointed to be over the entire state of North Carolina. So, in the summer of 1941, the great move was made to Greensboro, North Carolina

My father chose Greensboro because it was a college town and he saw that as an opportunity to continue his children's education in an academic, cultural environment. Although it was a very hot June, the adjustment to the new community and to the new school was smooth. My seventh grade homeroom teacher, Mrs. Ophelia Sharp Grandy, my favorite teacher, was the epitome of a classy, educated southern belle. Again, I was favored by the teacher and she recommended me to be the school announcer. History repeats itself! My northern accent was ridiculed. I was appointed the current event radio announcer for the grade school. My pronunciation of "boys" did not sound the same as my southern classmates, and they delighted in mocking me saying, "Good morning, boys and girls. May I have your attention, please?"

To add more insult to injury, my father's charismatic tent church service in an open field was another source of teasing. My mother played the guitar in the service, so my classmates would simulate playing an imaginary guitar and sing, "I am sanctified and holy," to mock my family and me,

If they intended to ridicule me, they were not successful because I really was not ashamed of being sanctified. I have never even really minded being called a *holy roller*. I had not read that scripture,

> For I am not ashamed of the gospel of Christ: for it
> is the power of God unto salvation to everyone that
> believeth; to the Jew first, and also to the Greek.
>
> Romans 1:16 (KJV)

I just was not ashamed of my father's preaching, the saints shouting and mother playing the guitar singing, *I Am a Soldier in the Army of the Lord.* My mother and father loved me and took good care of me, and I appreciated them and I loved them right back. So, that was that! My friends hollered and jumped around at the local football games, without shame. I concluded that hollering in church for Jesus, seemed to me, to be a better cause. It was matter of choosing for whom you hollered.

I did, and still have, a real fear of chickens. When this became known, people raised them in their yards and they walked around the neighborhood yards, the students would threaten to put a chicken on me. It was divine providence that got Ruth Curtis to volunteer to protect me. Mother promised her a nickel, but we became friends and she protected me gratis.

Although we are miles apart, Ruth Curtis Jackson McLean and I have remained friends for over seventy years, and we continue to remember birthdays and holidays.

High school was fun. The drama class enhanced my academic program and I had the lead actress role in every production from my sophomore until my senior year. The greatest reward was for receiving the 1946 Best Actress Award for the Colored Schools in North Carolina in Raleigh, the capital, during my senior year. This would not have occurred had it not been for the faithful support of my late drama teacher, Mrs. Barbara Johnson Wells (no kin), and my mother. Mother traveled with me during local and state oratorical contests and bolstered my self-confidence in my dramatic talent. In fact, mother was an enabling supporter for most of my academic achievements.

Mother always stayed involved in our education. She also continued this practice for some of the grandchildren She always attended Parent and Teachers Association (P.T.A.) meetings. My father was determined to earn a good living so that we could have a good home environment, and mother was determined to develop scholars with some class. Hold our head up high and be somebody, was still her motto.

My father traveled a lot conducting revivals, but Mother kept the home and stayed in touch with the teachers throughout my grade and high school years.

My father also encouraged our studying and I'll never forget that he once sat up all night with me, until I completed writing a term paper.

Parent involvement had its rewards. My high school diploma was awarded to me when I was sixteen; my Bachelor of Arts degree at twenty; my Masters of Arts degree at twenty-three, and I began to pursue my doctoral degree soon thereafter.

THE OVEN GETS HOT

Earlier, you were told about my outgoing, friendly personality. Well, it got me into trouble when I was sixteen years old.

During my senior year in high school, I was standing with a close friend of mine on the bus stop waiting for the bus for school. A very handsome man in an army sergeant's uniform approached us and spoke with familiarity. When I asked my friend, "Who is that?"

She responded, "My Uncle Jack."

"Hello, Uncle Jack." was my immediate salutation.

This salutation caused him to turn around and ask, "Who is this pretty young lady?"

"Claudia." was my friend's response.

"Hi, Darling." He replied, while looking me up and down.

We boarded the bus, and I did not give it another thought. The Saints would have said that I was just being fast, meaning too aggressive.

Uncle Jack arranged to meet me and a clandestine romance began almost immediately.

The difference in our ages was obvious, but it was much later when it became known that he was the same age as my mother. By then it was too late. I was smitten and mesmerized by his suave mannerisms and worldly expressions. This worldly, dark, handsome man looked like a black version of Caesar Romero, and I fell, foolishly in love.

It was not easy to keep this romance a well kept secret. Our clandestine affair was almost discovered several times.

One evening when my parents were attending a weekly prayer, I called by telephone and invited Jack to sneak to our home and meet me on the back porch.

I really became uneasy as soon as he arrived. "Jack, something tells me that you had better leave." was my greeting.

"I just got here." he protested.

"I don't care. Please, just leave." I pleaded.

As soon as Jack had cleared our driveway, my father's car headlights penetrated the darkness. That was a close call. I ran upstairs and hurriedly joined my brother and sister who were in bed already asleep.

The next day, in a casual conversation, I overheard Miss Irene, our neighbor, mention to my mother that she might have been seeing things, but she thought that she had seen a man last night in our back yard.

Not taking the remark too seriously, Mother politely replied, "I hope not."

I sweated and perspired, too. Boy, all hell would break loose if my parents even suspected the truth, and to have this man in the house!

Oblivious to my unscrupulous plan, my father had begun a special savings account for my medical school tuition. I always, from an early age, wanted to be a gynecologist and obstetrician. That was my ultimate career goal until the devil got into the plan. By the time that I was seventeen, Jack had convinced me that we should elope immediately after my eighteenth birthday, January 17, 1948.

Meanwhile, at sixteen, I had enrolled in Bennett College, a prestigious all girls Methodist college. The president, the late Dr. David Dallas Jones, was a very strict administrator. The girls' behaviors were closely monitored. We were required to attend vesper everyday and to sit in our assigned seats. Attendance was taken, and over two cuts were prohibited. Additionally, emphasis was placed on public decorum and appearance. The co-eds were required to wear a hat and gloves when leaving the campus and were never allowed to leave the campus alone. None of my co-ed friends were married, and I was not too anxious to change my ability to have a good time and hang out at Webster's hamburger restaurants with my friends.

When my eighteenth birthday approached, I had some doubts as to whether or not I was going to go on with this marriage plan. It seemed glamorous at first, but the closer it got to my birthday, the less glamorous it seemed. To tell the truth, I got cold feet, but I felt that it would be necessary to reveal this romance to my parents in order for me to back out, and I was afraid to tell them. I had slipped most of my clothes out of my parents' home into Jack's house. I could not figure out how to return them without my plan being revealed.

On January 24, 1948, one week after my eighteenth birthday, Jack Hunt got a friend to drive me and a female friend so that he and I could elope in Mocksville, North Carolina. I had to use my ration book to ascertain my age at the Court House and the clerk was hesitant to issue us a marriage license. There was no turning back once the plan was put into motion. I became Mrs. Jack Lamont Hunt.

It grieves me now, to this very day, to recall my father's reaction when we first came face to face. My father cried again. If I could have turned back the clock, I would have. Too many people had been hurt by my elopement.

Within a few weeks, while preparing to go on a trip, my father had a heart attack. My mother suffered no less. She cried constantly and called me on the telephone hourly for days saying, "Claudia, why?" I believed that I was in love, but Tina Turner probably said it best, *What's Love Got to do with It?*" This marriage already was not worth breaking my parents' hearts. The Wells Family became temporarily dysfunctional.

I was afraid that going to the hospital to see my father would distress him further. So, I would just call the hospital desk every day to inquire, "Please tell me what you can about Rev. Wells' condition." This was years before we had the Privacy Law. The reports and prognosis given were generally favorable.

Before the heart attack, my father had taken drastic actions that included forbidding me to associate with my brother or sister. I missed my brother, O.T., more than anyone. This was too much for me to endure. Within two or three weeks after my father's recovery, I relented and I went to church one Sunday morning. I was so nervous, but simply overjoyed to be in the room with my family and the Saints.

When my father got up to give his sermon, he acknowledged my presence and requested me to come down front to the altar. I gladly and humbly complied.

After I had reached the altar, my father officially announced my marriage to the congregation, asked me my last name and publicly apologized for saying that he was disinheriting me. He slowly came down, stood beside me and asked the church to pray for our healing. The Amen's and Hallelujahs permeated the service. There seemed to have been lots of joy in that sanctified church that Sunday morning, as the church appeared to be on one accord and ready to begin the healing process.

I was happy to hug my mother and jubilant to be reunited with my brother, sister. and church friends. I felt that, God was in His heaven, and that all was right with the world.

Wait until I go home and tell this good news to Jack!

Jack received the news gladly and within days we visited my parents at the house together. I could have and would have spent the night, had we been invited.

Jack gave my mother and father the highest respect and slowly and cautiously won their acceptance. Even though he was as mature as they, he addressed them as, Mama and Daddy. Jack had not lost the smoothness that I first noticed that day on the bus stop. He was readily accepted by the Saints and my friend. He attended my church and became Brother Hunt.

The masquerade was short lived and, Jack soon began displaying jealousy. The age difference was, perhaps, a contributing factor. I could not be outgoing or talk to anyone without being at first criticized, later scolded and finally physically abused. In fact, I became accustom to the physical abuse. I was battered two or three times a week. Once, in the bathroom, he came in and hit me so hard I fell into the bathtub and the free standing tub became dislodged from the pipes. I never offered resistance or sought help. I was afraid that it would get worse.

Once, when a young minister was attending one of my father's conventions, Jack and I volunteered to house him as a delegate. As soon as the delegate had retired to his room, Jack began accusing me of secretly dating him. No denial could save me from being hit, so to keep the disturbance from being heard by our visitor, I stayed on the outdoor back steps all night. The next day my mother asked me,

"Claudia, why do you look so tired. Have you been crying?"

I did not respond. I stood silently and dropped my head. She shook her head in disgust and walked away.

Physical abuse was witnessed by my neighbors and my associates. Later, when I showed my father the broken bathtub, my father told Jack, "Son, if you keep hitting my daughter, you are going to make me sin." Jack would delight in privately repeating that statement to his sister and close friends. He seemed amused.

Our relationship was off and on. Later, things got a little better, and on February 18, 1949, Jack and I had a darling baby boy, Thaddeus Raydell Hunt, the joy of the family, and the apple of Jack's eye. Thaddeus was named for my beloved brother, Ozro Thaddeus, better known as O.T.

The birth of our son and the first grandson brought happiness into the Wells and Hunt households. Jack was so proud of his son, and spent a lot of time walking and playing with him. Jack was extremely attentive to his son and lavished him with love.

We lived in an integrated neighborhood because Jack, a veteran, was allowed to purchase a house wherever he could afford. It just so happened that our house was across the street from a city park for Whites Only. This restriction was a source of annoyance and embarrassment to Jack. One day, after Thaddeus had cried to go on a swing that he could see in the park, Jack grabbed him up, walked defiantly into the park, and said, "You can swing, son. Your daddy fought for this country." After that, late in the evening after the park had closed, he would take his son and let him play on the sliding board for a few minutes in the dark, segregated park. I stayed home, peeped out of the window and prayed. Jack was willing to die to give his son this privilege. They say that God protects babies and fools. I believed that one of each was in the park.

Like I said, from the very beginning, "Teddy", as Thaddeus was called, was the apple of everyone's eye. Jack had very little money and no insurance. My mother and my father had to pay the hospital bill, so when my mother came to take me home from the hospital, she gave the ambulance driver her home address. This assured her that my new son and I would be at her home for thirty days? Women stayed indoors thirty days, then, after giving birth. The Wells Family was delighted; Jack Hunt was outdone. I had mixed emotions. At least, I would have plenty of help with my new parenting responsibility and I could avoid abuse.

DeOla and O.T. insisted on sharing time with Teddy. DeOla coaxed him to call out, frantically, "Aunt Dee!" whenever he assumed that he was in trouble. O.T., for whom he was named, took him with him to Bennett College on his dates and taught him, as soon as he could talk, to call the pretty coeds Young Tender or Red Bone, if they had fair complexions.

There was momentary peace when we returned home but this did not last long. Jack had already insisted that I change my pre-med major as he was not going to allow me to go to Meharry Medical College and be separated from him. My father did not know about this change in my future plans. He was still saving monthly for me to attend medical school. Therefore, it was a major disappointment when I was awarded a Bachelor of Arts degree from Bennett College '50, instead of a Bachelor of Science degree at my commencement. My parents did not know, until my commencement. I had hurt my parents again. I had a husband, an infant son, a degree and the promise of a bleak future.

In the meantime, my marriage was becoming more volatile and complicated. Jack was a philanderer and the other women began calling me to ascertain that I was sharing my husband with them. One of them, with whom he was spending a lot of time, was invited by me, when she called me, to come to our home and repeat what she was assuring me about their romantic escapades. I invited her to arrive a little before the exact time when I knew that Jack would come home for his lunch.

When his girlfriend arrived, I had to admit that she was attractive. She was of a fair complexion with hazel eyes, tall, thin and stylishly dressed. If there were fault to be found, it would have been that she was very heavily made up, especially with rouge. After seeing her, I wished that I had put on my best dress and maybe a little powder or lipstick. To add insult to injury, I recognized her to be the sister of one of our close male friends. Oh, well.

Imagine Jack's surprise when he walked into the house and saw me sitting totally relaxed in the living room with one of his girlfriends.

"What are you doing here?" he rudely asked.

Before she could respond, I quickly replied," I asked her to come to tell me again that you plan to leave me for her."

Infuriated, Jack grabbed her, slapped her and proceeded to forcefully push her out of the door. I quietly sat and observed the fracas between them. It was disgusting to see

43

how he manhandled her. There was no joy to be taken from this volatile, ugly scene, especially watching your husband physically abusing a woman.

When he had succeeded in getting her out of the door, I got up, without saying a word, packed my baby's bottle and blanket, and left him sitting stunned in the living room chair. It appeared that his lunch had been served too hot for him to digest.

Mr. and Mrs. Jack Lamont Hunt and son, Thaddeus

JUMPING HURDLES AND MOVING ON

I minored in dramatics and won recognition in high school and in college. I was recommended by my college drama instructor and I accepted a minor role in a local Off-Broadway Summer Round Theater. Because the company was all Caucasian, this stirred Jack's ire and jealousy to its highest.

It did not matter to him that my being the first and only black with this company performing to a southern audience was breaking a precedent. You see, the Coloreds were not allowed to attend the local round theater playhouse because it did not have a balcony in which to segregate. After I had established my thespian talent, a few days before the scheduled performance of *The Little* Foxes, I refused to perform as Addie, unless they at least allow the Coloreds to attend dress rehearsal. They had made the mistake of not getting me an understudy. They reluctantly consented. I had set a precedent, and Jack attended the dress rehearsal.

My performance as a thespian was warmly applauded by the audience, and on opening night, an after party was held for the cast at a posh home in an exclusive suburb of Greensboro. Naturally, Jack was invited to accompany me. He was rather surly, but polite during the party.

My association and familiarity with the white actors really infuriated Jack and he abused me both physically and verbally as soon as we got home. It was his practice, if he was displeased, to hit me on my head, as soon as we got into the door. I generally could tell when it was coming to me and would prepare to defend myself by throwing my arm up to protect my eyes. I seldom fought back, because when I did, his fury would increase.

Additionally, he would verbally abuse me with vulgarity. It was too much to endure when my toddler son began repeating the vulgar verbal abuse that he was hearing. This was more than I was willing to endure. I decided to get out before somebody got hurt. Remember what happened to Joseph Range when he backed me in a corner?" I felt like I was in another corner, and something had to be done.

I had previously become accustomed to having a black eye and bruises, and no longer tried to sequester myself or stay out of the public's eye. Many inquisitive who already had an idea what had happened would ask me, "Claudia, what's wrong with your eye or what happened to your arm?"

"Jack hit me." Was my only response. I was already hurt, and the fact they knew could not hurt me anymore. Nevertheless, I was very tired of being abused! Enough is enough!!!!!! Involving our son is the last straw; plus my son is learning abuse from his father whom he dearly loved. I have got to get out of this hell hole. Soon.

There was a brief reprieve when I got my first job teaching in a small town in eastern North Carolina about three hours ride from Greensboro. My parents gladly kept Thaddeus and I would come home every other weekend. At first, the separation just made the weekends with Jack somewhat pleasurable. I later learned that, while I was away, he was having a great time with his other women. The pleasure did not last long and the jealousy and the physical abuse escalated. I was resolute in my earlier opinion that enough is enough!

I was not going to take it anymore. I bought a gun, some bullets and showed it to Jack. He did not seem to be disturbed and kind of brushed it off with a threatening remark. I hid the gun. To further set him on notice that I was not going to take his abuse anymore, one Sunday afternoon while he was asleep in the spare bedroom, I set the bed on fire. If I had not awakened him, I might have served a jail sentence for murder. This loving, warm, outgoing, friendly young lady had turned bitter and dangerous. I hated Jack! I despised looking at him. If he would touch me or try to embrace me, I would let out a scream and I rejected his amorous advances. His attempt at love making was rejected.

I was displeased with the person that I had become. I wanted out! I took my precious son, Thaddeus, my Doberman Pincher, a few of the clothes that my parents had bought me, a set of china and silverware that my father had given me for a college graduation present, and I got out of that hell hole and did not look back. Goodbye, Jack, forever.

Jack began stalking me and tearfully begging me to give him another chance to change his behavior. No chance. I had had enough. So, one morning, after discussing that my son and my Doberman Pincher would be alright at my parents', my father suggested and bought me a one way ticket on a train to Washington, D.C. and that ended the love story of Jack and Claudia. A strong woman arrived in the capital.

"Like the poet said, "My head is bloody, but unbowed.""

STRUTTING MY FREEDOM IN THE CITY

Living in Washington, D.C. was a great change of life style. I was free! I was on my own for the first time in my life, and it all seemed so glamorous. I shared a swank, contemporary apartment on Kansas Avenue, N.W., with two single young ladies. There was so much for me learn about my new found freedom. I felt that I was a character in a Soap Box Series, *One Life to Live* or *Search for Tomorrow*.

I was smart enough to align myself with a church whose minister was a friend of my father. This turned out to be a source of nurturing because I was reunited with some North Carolinians with whom there had been a distant relationship, and someone always invited me to their home for dinner after Sunday morning worship. In reality, I was living in an urban environment with small town ways. In retrospect, I sometimes invited myself for dinner or visited without an invitation. It was not necessary, where I had lived, to call someone before visiting, you just showed up, stayed for hours, and stayed for dinner, if invited. That was called Southern Hospitality.

It took me several weeks to find a job, but eventually, I was hired for a job in the main library, District of Columbia Public library. I was assigned to inspect and repair rental B'nai B'rith film. This was easy enough and I managed, seemingly, to please my supervisor. I had finally found peace in the alcove of the library, far from the crowd.

There was a young Jewish lawyer working part time in the library who was waiting to take the bar exam. He began coming to my station during his lunch time and at every break to talk to me. I was ambivalent to the attention that he was giving to me. My recent experience had left me with no desire to get involved romantically with any man. I was just happy and free, at last.

Months later, upon my arrival, one Monday morning, I was summoned to the supervisor's office. This did not cause any anxiety as I had been told by my supervisor that I was doing a good job. Maybe a promotion or a transfer to the floor was going to be offered. It was sometimes lonely in that dark alcove. I happily went into the conference room.

The meeting was short and abrupt. My service was no longer needed! There was not really any attempt to answer my question or to give me a reason. Just, your service is no longer needed, period. Clear the premises!

I was stunned. While gathering up my belongings out of the locker, my Jewish friend came down to tell me that he, too, had just been released from his part time duties. What a coincidence!

We just said a few polite parting words, parted and went our separate ways. I was more concerned about what I was going to tell my roommates or my parents. I was embarrassed because I had been fired. So, I led my roommates to believe that I was still working. I got up every morning and rode the bus seeking employment elsewhere.

Finally, after many futile attempts to find suitable employment, I told my parents that I had been released from my job because of President Eisenhower's reduction in force known as the RIF. Odd jobs could not pay my part of the rent, I had to return home. My parents received me with love and open arms. Thomas Wolfe had not met my parents when he wrote the novel, *You Can't Home Again*.

Meanwhile, Jack had moved to New York and was no longer a threat to me. At last, I was safe. I was pleased to be reunited with my son who had become precocious, with his new playmate, Billy.

A SUMMER IN THE BIG APPLE

Returning home after spending a year in a metropolitan environment was boring, so I went to New York to look for a job for the summer. I arrived in New York knowing few people except a few church people. It was certain that I had no intentions of seeing or reuniting with Jack. Initially, I spent a few nights with a Greensboro friend until a room was available at the YWCA on 38th and Lexington Avenue, in the heart of Manhattan.

My lodging was a small room overlooking 38th Street. There was bustle and activity all around me, but I was not a part of it and I was lonely. My interest turned to spending a great amount of the time looking out of the window. Interestingly enough, this young, colored girl, Nora, who also lived in the "Y" was dating this young, Caucasian man who sat outside in his car all evening seemingly waiting for Nora to come out after she returned from work. I had never witnessed anything so bizarre. Out of curiosity, I struck up a conversation with her to perhaps have someone with whom to associate and to satisfy my window curiosity.

New Yorkers appear to be rather private, but Nora welcomed my conversations and we would sit in the parlor and read The New York Times together. She seemed oblivious that her friend was parked outside in his car waiting for her. Finally, after we had had several conversations, I asked her,

"Do you know that your friend is parked outside?" I asked her for the sole purpose of being just plain nosey.

"Oh, yes. He waits for me while I am home." She casually replied. A later conversation revealed that he was a practicing attorney from a very wealthy family.

My private thought was wouldn't it be nice to have someone wealthy to sit patiently for hours and wait for me. Then a small voice said, "Suppose it was Jack?" Yes, I thought, that is just another form of control. No thanks.

Tambourines to Glory was playing on Broadway and my friend had a musical role in it. Additionally, I previously knew this friend from Memphis and he and I attended the same church in New York. Our friendship was quickly renewed and it was refreshing to get out the "Y" window watching the pathetic scene of Nora's boyfriend wait in his car to be at her beckoning call.

It was just wonderful being invited to my friend's apartment. He always had some thespian, musician or someone there. His apartment was sparsely furnished but lively. Someone would volunteer to go and to get some "take out' food from the deli. I loved the liverwurst sandwiches,

I really felt like a city girl when I was in their presence. Granted, I did not understand everyone making so many trips into the bathroom. The bathroom appeared to be the agreed gathering place.

Usually, it was occupied and when the person would come out they would ask, "Does anyone want to come in?"

"Yeah, man." my friend or one of his guest would eagerly respond.

The bathroom stayed so busy, so, I never tried to use it. It probably was not clean enough for me with so many men using it. I was still Mama's child and liked cleanliness.

One weekend while I was visiting, someone was in the bathroom heaving so loudly that I could hear him in the front room. My friend opened the bathroom door and I could see that it was the musician. My friend grabbed the musician around the waist while he was heaving to keep his head from going down into the commode. Wanting to help, I offered to call emergency or an ambulance, as we called it then.

"No, girl. Get out of here and mind your business." was my friend's harsh response.

My feelings were hurt and I realize that being in this apartment was worse than looking out of the "Y" window. I made up some flimsy excuse and left to go back to 38th and Lexington. Who wanted to eat a deli sandwich while someone was vomiting?

My friend seemed not to care that I was abruptly leaving, and closed the bathroom door, in a good riddance gesture.

On Monday morning, it was a pleasure returning to my new job at Saks Fifth Avenue on 5th and Lexington. I, a neophyte to New York, had been lucky to get the job as an attendant in the dressing rooms for the Edith Lancer's Salon, located in Saks Fifth Avenue.

My persistence had gotten me the job. When I applied for employment, I was told that there was a job available in the Edith Lancer Salon, but since my application indicated that I had not previously worked in New York, they could not hire me.

My retort was, "How can I work in New York if someone does not have enough faith in me to give me my first chance?"

There was a pregnant pause. "If I gave you a chance, tomorrow is the 4th of July, when could you start?"

"Right now," I said without hesitating.

"Report tomorrow to the fifth floor, right wing. Good Luck. Oh, by the way, you are a dressing room attendant and you must wear a black dress every day. Do you have one?"

Without thinking, I said, "I'll get one." followed by several, "Thank, you's"

My thought was, Okay, Claudia, you did it.! New York, I am here!

Edith Lancer had leased a section of the fifth floor of Saks Fifth Avenue and made custom lingerie, particularly, bras for women with mastectomies. I had never before heard the word *mastectomy*. Breast cancer was not discussed openly, and very little was available for prosthetic needs. This service at Edith Lancer's was very expensive and mainly used by the wealthy women, like eastside residents or wives of stars or movie producers. Activity in the salon was always in a private dressing room. Who came and what transpired were forbidden to be discussed by clerks and/or dressing room attendants.

I enjoyed the exclusive aspects of it, and made such a positive impression that I was offered part time employment indefinitely. This offer, however, was not enough to keep me for a winter in that small YWCA room looking out of the window. So, again, I headed back home to Greensboro to my family.

BACK TO MY ROOTS

The following fall, I desperately again sought employment as a teacher. When I became discouraged, a handyman who did odd jobs for my father saw me sitting looking despondent. He inquired about my unhappy look, and when I told him that I was sad because I was unable to find a teaching job, he said, "Well, my daughter got a letter about a job, but she has already taken one. I'll go home and get the letter." He returned within hours and I was able to apply, interview and to be hired to my first teaching assignment in Winterville, North Carolina.

Roberta Flack, who later became a renowned singer, was the music teacher in the adjoining town, Pine Tops, in the same Pitt County School System where I had been hired as librarian/English Instructor. The black teachers' Pitt County meetings were held separately from the white Pitt County teachers meeting. Roberta and I met in the same meetings.

Winterville was nestled between two main tobacco towns, Greenville and Ayden. The main source of income was tobacco farming and tobacco factory work. The whites farmed and made all of the money; the blacks harvested and worked in the factory. The town was very segregated with Colored and White Only water fountains and dingy, segregated waiting rooms in the bus station that I frequently had to use.

Once my young son was in the car and begged to buy an ice cream cone from a Dairy Queen stand on the Wilson highway. I was embarrassed and reluctant to counter his persistent request with the fact that black people could not buy ice cream from that stand. Soon, I hesitatingly relented, parked the car a little away from the front of the stand, gave him some money and told him, "Go get it."

He happily jumped out of the car, got on his tiptoes at the stand's window and I heard him ask the young, white female, "Can I please have one dip of ice cream?"

She responded, "We don't serve coloreds."

Not comprehending, he replied, "I don't want chocolate. I want banilla."

Perhaps she was amused or became momentarily compassionate when she responded, "I'll serve you this time, but don't come back, now you hear. "White Southerners often ended a sentence with, "now you hear."

He happily returned to the car licking his ice cream. I did not say a word. I just drove back onto the highway, and continued our trip.

It was difficult to be in this environment and maintain high self esteem. I, too found myself frequently testing the system. There were numerous incidents.

One that comes immediately to mind is a quiet fall, Saturday afternoon. I had driven a short distance to do some shopping. A State Patrolman appeared at my door within minutes of my return home. When I answered, he came in without being invited. He immediately stated that he had seen me driving my Thunderbird and that he called to check my license plate and discovered that I did not have auto insurance. This surprised me as my father paid my automobile insurance, and he was very prompt with his bills. I informed the State Patrolman that I would have to make a long distance call to my father to ascertain the information.

Whereupon, the Patrol said," Girl, we can settle this here and now. All you have to do is to give me some and I'll forget the whole thing and won't arrest you." This infuriated me, but I needed to restrain myself for my safety. Fools rush in where angels dare to tread. Being a fool could very well be costly as my son was at a neighbor's playing and I was home alone.

My reply was simply and rather quietly, "I don't pay insurance premiums with my body. So, please leave." Needless to say, I was trembling and anxious as to what his response would be.

He sort of snarled paused for a moment, looked me straight in my face and responded, "I could kill you, Nigger, dump you and no one would know or find you."

"Yes", I said defiantly," but if you touch me, we both are going to wake up in hell 'cause I am going to fight you right back."

He said simply, "You are a spunky little nigger", turned and walked out of the door.

I had stood up for my rights and I had preserved my dignity and survived! Whew!!! Hold your head up high and be somebody. My heart almost beat out of the walls of my chest.

This colored, rural educational environment was different than any that I had heard about. The school was micro-managed. The teachers, locals, were very comfortable with the unusual practice of selling food in the classroom to raise money for the annual rally. The teachers were given an amount to be raised and to be turned over to the administration. I began to question my colleagues about the purpose of this practice. They strongly advised me to comply if I wanted to keep my job. When I confided in them that I was not going to raise any money, they nervously got together and sold oranges in the classroom to raise my money. They liked me, my urban dress and lifestyle, and did not want me to get terminated.

At the end of the school year, the principal came to my class room with a typewriter and asked me if I wanted my contract renewed for the next year. The contracts were renewed annually. When I expressed my desire to return the next year, he told me to type a letter of resignation from my present assignment as librarian/ English Instructor. He explained that since I had been hired in his wife's position, who was presently on a maternity leave, that in order to be reassigned, I had to vacate my present position. I did not quite understand the rationale, but I reluctantly complied.

The principal's wife returned to her job, and I was left seeking employment again. I later fully understood why it was necessary for me to resign.

My subsequent positions exposed me to myriad experiences, both pleasant and unpleasant in the North Carolina Public Education System. I taught at Newbold High School in Lincolnton, North Carolina, and Charles H. Darden High School in Wilson, North Carolina, which are both well-managed schools. Also, I was given a strong instructional foundation at the James B. Dudley High School, the high school from which I had graduated. It was interesting becoming colleagues to my former instructors. My respect for them made it difficult for me to accept them as peers, but they insisted and took me under their professional wings. I was warmly received and they shared excellent teaching strategies with me.

I was appointed as a teacher at James B. Dudley High School immediately after my father spoke to the principal. There are perks and handicaps from your parents being well connected. Most of the time it worked in my favor, occasionally, it precluded my adult, professional privacy, as was the case of my father and the principal. My principal would remind me, after even a minor infraction, that he was,"…going to speak to Reverend about this."

While in Greensboro, I was again in my parents' home with my son, which left me some advantages and time to do further study. Through summer study I was able to attain my Masters of Arts Degree and to pursue my doctoral degree.

I also received scholarships to the University of Oslo, Oslo, Norway; to Indiana State University, Terre Haute, Indiana. However, my Mother's illness prevented my taking advantage of my University of Oslo Scholarship.

One summer school rekindles an unpleasant memory. My experience pursuing my doctorate degree (1962) Duke University, a southern ivy-league university, was a humiliating experience. I was a first black doctoral candidate, and my presence seemed neither welcomed by my advisor, my instructors, nor some of the student body.

I applied for a semi-private dormitory room. This was a wise decision, as I was alone and had the amenities of a private room. Alone again! I was alone, and the colored maids gave me every extra service possible. Yes, the dormitory had maids who changed your linen, cleaned your room and delivered the mail on silver trays.

I learned the meaning of isolation, but I remembered to always to hold your head up high and be somebody. A few girls would study with me, but when their relatives or friends would visit them on the weekend, they would shun me, walk by me and turn their heads to avoid speaking or recognizing me. Being ignored was not too bad; having everyone get up from the table in the cafeteria or hearing them say, "Let's move. We don't want to eat watermelon." did not cause me too much concern, either. The greatest challenge was when I would walk through the campus from the cafeteria to my dormitory.

The male summer school undergraduates, a goodly number of whom reportedly, had failed a course or two during the regular semester, would line the walkway, hoot and taunt me, this post graduate student.

One day an undergraduate said, "Here comes the baboon."

"What are you going to do with her?" was the question posed.

"Give her a banana." was the response.

"No, stick it in her ear."

Someone added, "I'll stick my d— in her ear." This remark was followed by loud laughter.

Hold my head up high and walk by them was my intention. But that day, I stopped, looked the nearest one of them in the eye and said, "Hi, what have I done to you?"

His face flushed and he dropped his head.

> A soft answer turneth away wrath: but grievous words
> stir up anger.
>
> Proverbs 15:1(KJV)

I seldom like to recall the summer of 1962, but the question asked by me that day seemed to have caused the taunting to quickly subside. I grew my first gray hair that summer. The pressure was great, and the odds were stacked against me. I needed to find an easier way to become Dr. Claudia Wells Hunt, but I finished the summer with my head held high, whole, undefeated with my personal dignity. I could have presented them valid proof that indicated that I was being treated and graded unfairly, but it would have been difficult to substantiate beyond a reasonable doubt. Nevertheless, my presence had set a precedent. There had to be a better way to pursue a doctoral degree, and I found it. I put the summer of 1962 behind me, and moved on to the University of North Carolina, Chapel Hill.

For over fifty years, I have kept, in my wallet as a trophy, my laminated library stack permit card issued June 18, 1962, only to PhD. Candidates, English, Carrel S43.

THE STRUGGLE TO OVERCOME

In 1964, Woolworth Drug Store, Greensboro, North Carolina, was the site in which another change of the civil rights history of America began. It was where the sit-ins began. Three young black A. & T. State College students were aware of some long-standing injustices practiced in the south, and decided that they were not going to take it anymore. In fact, my son, Thaddeus and Sheila Blair, the sister of one of the original three, recalled an incident at the ice cream store that created the urgency for the immediate beginning of the pre- planned sit-in.

Jesse Jackson was senior class president at A&T. College and joined the original three in the leadership for this protest against segregation in the eating places. A.&T. Students, Bennett College Students, high school students, clergy and adults united in this historical sit-in and march. Bishop Wells and other religious leaders also joined this historical movement.

I had returned to my high school alma mater as a teacher and because of my son, Thaddeus, and Billy's very active involvement, I got caught up immediately in the spirit of the protest. In fact, the majority of the black population was caught up in the movement. As soon as school was dismissed, I would put on my tennis shoes and join the thousands of young and old blacks marching on the streets of Greensboro singing, *We Shall Overcme*. There was a foreboding, eerie mood over the city. The whites were angry and resistant; the blacks determined and relentless.

"What do ya'll colored people want? "was the question asked by the Chief of Police.

"We want our freedom like everybody else." was the resounding response.

My family and I would be doing our Christmas shopping, and it was impossible to even get a sandwich from one of the restaurants. Fast food restaurants weren't around. We would have to stop shopping, get in the car and go home to eat and then return to resume shopping.

Meanwhile, white shoppers would be lined up at K& W Cafeteria waiting to go in for lunch or dinner. The aroma of food was whetting the appetite, but it was impossible for my family and me to eat there. It was almost impossible to not fully realize that you were not a part of this great democracy for which the Civil War had been fought.

We would clap our hands and sing enthusiastically, "Deep in my heart, I do believe, we shall overcome someday." This melody of hope filled the air on Elm and Market Streets. Cry for freedom was in the air. You could feel the tenseness all over the city.

We want our freedom and our American rights! We shall overcome someday was the prevailing attitude.

My son, Thaddeus, and Billy, who was Jesse Jackson's cellmate, along with thousands of young students and adults went to jail for trying to buy a ticket to enter the main lobby of the White Only theater. They received inhumane treatment. People would spit in the faces of protestors, and racial slurs and the word, nigger, were prevalent. There seemed to be no recognition or regard that black people were human beings with feelings. The spirit of all men being created equal was moot.

When Mother insisted that I go and sign Billy out of jail, Billy would plead with me to include his cellmate, Jesse. All that I was required to do is to sign saying that I would accept responsibility that he would appear when a court date was set.

"No. I can't be responsible for Jesse." was my answer. On hindsight that was, indeed, a mistake because he was not a flight risk, and his mother lived in South Carolina. There wasn't anyone to sign for him.

Jesse Jackson emerged and remains a highly respected leader in the Civil Rights Movement. His voice is heard and respected around the world. I wish that I could have had the foresight to match my hindsight. Maybe it would have been Billy who would have had to wait.

Thaddeus emerged as a leader for crowd control. He organized his fellow detainees to repeat the Declaration of Independence, The Preamble to the Constitution over and over to the annoyance of the sheriffs on duty. When the family was later told what he had done, we were proud of Thaddeus, and also of Billy for their major contributions to our civil rights.

Because Thaddeus was a minor, an officer had to personally take him home to deliver him to an adult. The secret tactic of the parents was to turn off the house lights and not answer the doorbell until several attempts had been made. The officer had to make a personal delivery of a minor to the parent, according to the law. This delay tactic caused an inconvenience and required patrol overtime, thus impacting on the fiscal budget.

"Reverend, your grandson was arrested attempting to break the law today and was taken into custody. Charges have not yet been filed, so I am returning him to you and asking you to please keep him home."

"I'll do what I can, Officer," was my father's nonconvincing answer.

Patience was wearing thin, the officers were on twenty-four hour duty and it was not unusual to see an officer asleep on duty standing against a telephone post. Additionally, the overtime was putting a strain on the city's budget. Rumor had it that overtime for one month had used up the annual law enforcement budget.

The atmosphere was tense! Could there be violence?

The situation was also loaded. One evening during the march, I had decided to volunteer to be arrested to chaperone the young people in jail. It was still being reported that the policemen on duty in the holding areas were putting the young boys and girls together and encouraging them to have sex. So, adults were allowing themselves to be arrested to chaperone. As I lifted my foot to get on the Arrest Bus, a student hollered out of the bus window, "No, Mrs. Hunt, don't get on the bus. They need you at school." If you wanted to go to jail, all you had to do was get on the bus when the policeman would holler, "You're under arrest!" Students would run and voluntarily get on the bus. Had it not been for the student, I, too, would have been arrested. I stayed off of the busses and just marched until my feet became calloused.

It was a long and bitter fight, but the history books will prove that, we did overcome and changed the profile of the United States of America.

Consequently, I emerged from the sit-ins tough and eager to put my personal pain behind me and to make an impact on the world, and most especially to develop a lasting love and interest in young people.

After teaching in North Carolina for thirteen years and having the privilege of returning to my high school alma mater as a teacher of English, I decided to make a giant move.

In September, 1964, I moved to Detroit, Michigan, and became a part of the integration of Redford High School. With the Detroit Public Schools System, I proudly held positions as teacher of Honors English; department head of the English department; unit head of English and social studies, Post and Mettetal Jr. Highs; secondary assistant principal, M.L. King High School and Mettetal Middle School and Guest Middle School. I retired, in 1994, after forty-three years of total service, as a secondary high school principal, Southeastern High School.

In the interim, I experienced the bitter-sweet of a struggle for human dignity. However, the pleasant memories pale the struggle.

A BIG CHANGE

It was early November, an exciting time in the Wells' household because my parents were going to take their annual trip to the Holy Convocation in Memphis, Tennessee.

This was an especially joyous time for me as I was bursting with pride observing the positive influence that my father had on the delegates. He had charisma before the word became vogue. He also was successful in crowd control. He could stand before the convention and say, "My Dears, please be seated." and the crowd of thousands would take their seats immediately and give him their undivided attention. Many would marvel at this, as there were very few leaders who could control the crowd at the national convention in Memphis, Tennessee. My father was uniquely dynamic with a magnetic, charismatic personality.

1974, was not to be any different than the previous years. He had, as you might recall, had a heart attack in 1948, and later a paralyzing stroke in 1953. His health was in a slow decline, but he was staying active in both his capacities as a General Board Member of the Church of God in Christ, bishop of Greater North Carolina Ecclesiastical Jurisdiction and pastor respectively for two local Churches of God in Christ. So, just as a precaution, he checked himself into the hospital to get a physical examination and to address some minor health concerns. His clothes had been packed for the trip, the reservations had been made and the time for departure had come and gone. Mother was concerned that Daddy had insisted on remaining in the hospital, so she called me in Detroit and told me the situation. Whereupon, I volunteered to fly to Greensboro and to accompany my parents to Memphis. I had already planned to go to Memphis with my husband, Ernest, and my clothes were also packed for that trip. This only required a minor change of plans.

Upon my arrival in Greensboro, I went directly to the hospital where the family had gathered in a somewhat pseudo festive mood. Our younger brother, Billy, surreptitiously brought some food into the room for the family to have a bedside picnic. There was light chatter and small talk when suddenly my father indicated that he wanted to tell my mother goodbye. She adamantly rejected this, but after he had made several attempts, my sister, DeOla, stepped to the foot of the bed, volunteered and said, "Daddy, if you want somebody to say goodbye, I'll tell you goodbye."

This pleased him very much, and he must have symbolically passed his clergy mantle to DeOla. With the help of God, she spiritually picked the symbolic mantle up, so that it would not fall on the floor. Daddy raised his arms in praise to God. A deep silence fell in the room.

Seemingly, satisfied and relieved with her response, he began addressing the family individually and stating what he had tried to be to each. He said his good-byes, and peacefully prayed a touching family prayer. The family soon, thereafter, slowly, sadly left after I volunteered to spend the night as Daddy's night nurse. It seemed to appear that Daddy's condition was becoming critical and that a twenty-four hour vigil was needed.

Over in the night, quietly, almost inaudibly, Daddy began singing, *I Am Climbing High Mountains Trying to Get Home*, one of his favorites. Becoming too weak to sing, he asked me to sing. I gladly obliged. In my best soprano voice, strains of *Peace in the Valley*, another one of his favorites, melodiously filled the hospital room as the early morning sun began to peep over the horizon through his eastern window. I filled the air with music, and November 6, 1974, would to be a bright, cold, sunny day, if I had anything to do with it. I pulled back the draperies to let the sunshine bask the room.

Sadly, the sunshine was short lived in that room. Daddy's declining condition became apparent. He said that his feet were cold and asked for extra cover. Soon, thereafter, I discreetly phoned DeOla and suggested that she keep the children out of school and to come to the hospital.

When Daddy saw DeOla come into the room, he raised his head, looked, slumped over and breathed his last breath.

It appeared, Daddy had found his peace in the valley, but I did not want him to leave.

"DeOla, has he gone?" I asked.

DeOla gave an affirmative nod of the head and stood reverently by her father. She glanced down again at her watch and announced the time, "7:05."

I ran out of the room, let out a loud scream that alerted the station nurses. I collapsed to the floor in the hall screaming to the top of my voice, "It's over, it's over."

Hearing my distress, a Blue Code was soon called. I was on the floor and I could see legs running past me as one nurse said, "See about the lady on the floor."

DeOla had come into the hall, stood beside me on the floor and was urgently coaxing me, "Plucks, get up off the floor." Plucks is my nickname of endearment.

In my despair, I realized that Mother was on her way to the hospital, and not knowing that Daddy was on Blue Code and seeing me on the floor would be too much of a shock. So, I reluctantly, with DeOla's assistance, pulled myself up and sequestered myself into the telephone booth in the corridor. I immediately called my husband, Ernest, in Detroit for solace.

The situation became grave. Bishop J.O. Patterson and Bishop D.A. Burton, two of his best friends and colleagues, called from the national convention in Memphis to assure us that the Saints were praying for the Lord's will to be done.

Daddy had experienced a near death experience during an earlier illness, and requested that if he were ever near death again, not to pray him back. He would prefer to go on and be with his Lord. So be it.

Daddy was taken off of life support three days later with his son, O.T., his son-in-law, Ernest Travis, and our dear friend, George Hampton by his bedside. God gently took my beloved father into His bosom. On November 9, 1974, Wyoming Wells went to his eternal home.

THE BEGINNING OF THE CRUMBLING

The days and week that followed were sad. *The City Has Lost a Pastor* was the front page headline of the Greensboro Daily News. The city of Greensboro reverently observed Bishop Wyoming Wells' passing. On the day of his funeral, the bus route around the church, where the memorial was being held, was rerouted, and because Daddy and four other leading black men had opened the first full service bank by blacks, the banks all over Greensboro closed for one half hour during his memorial service. Also, directions were posted for persons arriving in the local airport.

At the memorial it was said that "He was a preacher's preacher" and ministers from every denomination in the city and the national Episcopal gave tribute to this holy and sanctified preacher, born on a pecan farm in Arkansas. Bishop Wyoming Wells established his ministry in North Carolina from a converted house on Small Alley, to a tent in a Good Samaritan's vacant field, and finally to a former

Presbyterian church with a pipe organ located on one of the main integrated thoroughfares of Greensboro.

The days, weeks and months that followed were traumatic My cheeks constantly burned from the salty tears that I shed. I lost so much weight within a week until the leather pants that I had worn on the plane when I arrived, actually fell off as I walked down the hall in my parents' home. The entire family was in deep grief and seclusion.

Time heals all wounds. It just takes longer for the deeper wounds, but this healing would take a long time.

A FLASHBACK TO THE MOTOR CITY

Is it merely a coincident or is it in the design of things that I first see my future husbands coming down the street. Remember, I met Jack on the bus stop with his niece.

The year or the date, I can't recall, but it was a hot, summer Sunday evening in the '50's, and we were trying to catch a breeze on the upper balcony of a two-family flat. I looked up and saw a tall, very handsome man coming down the street.

"Look at that good looking man coming down the street." I whispered to my sister as an aside.

Walter overheard me and said, "That's a friend of mine and he's coming to meet you, Claudia."

"Meet me?"

"Yes, he is one of my friends, and I invited him to come today to meet you." He chuckled.

We were introduced. Ernest Lee Travis. After some small talk, Walter suggested that we pack some blankets, some refreshments and go to spend the evening cooling off on Belle Isle.

Ernest was about the best looking man that I could ever remember knowing. He was over six feet tall, coffee brown complexion, silk, black hair and well groomed. I was overwhelmed by his good looks.

My son, Thaddeus, had accompanied me to Detroit to spend a few weeks with my sister and her family. It had been so hot in the kitchen that Sunday until we had delayed eating dinner. I rushed inside to quickly feed my son so that I could go on this blind date to Belle Isle. Instead, DeOla decided to pack the dinner and make a hasty picnic. Off to Belle Isle we went.

Ernest later complimented how well-behaved my son was on Belle Isle which made me feel more comfortable with him. My son was my pride and joy.

Ernest came to visit me almost every evening until it was time for Thaddeus and me to return to North Carolina. Just before leaving, Ernest mentioned that he was ready to get married. I did not take this to be a proposal. Anyway, I did not have such thoughts even though he was, indeed, one good looking dude.

In the first place, I did not think that I would ever marry again. Secondly, I did not know enough about Ernest. His poor grammar and his lack of education was a major deterrent for my having an interest in him. Also, Ernest was a cosmetologist in a local salon. I did not know if I wanted to deal with that stigma. So, I left old good looking Ernest Lee Travis and Detroit behind me.

Years later, in 1964, when I returned to Detroit, I learned that Ernest had married, had a daughter and was divorced.

Months later, I was again lonely and I looked him up in the telephone directory.

Well, Ernest had been married and seemed to be leading a "normal" life. Just maybe, I could give him a chance to prove himself.

Ernest seemed elated when I called, and came to visit me that very evening when he left work. We were reunited and within a month, began a courtship.

Ernest's good looks and pleasant disposition were recognized by most of my friends. In fact, quite a few of them became his customers. I decided that if he proved himself to be a man to me, I would accept him as a man, regardless of his profession.

Ernest and I had open discussions about the stigma of his profession. He was very concerned about the stigma that he had and was experiencing. In fact, when an anonymous man once hollered into the salon, "All you men in there are sissies.", Ernest became very disturbed and came to tell me that he was going to quit his job.

Repeatedly, I would say, "Ernest you know who you are and what you are. Knowing that should give you confidence in how you conduct yourself." This remark seemed to have bolstered his self-esteem.

I always reminded him that his associations and mannerisms would speak very loudly perhaps drowning out what he was saying or denying.

My divorce from Jack Hunt was final, and time had passed so quickly until it did not seem like sixteen years.

About three years after our renewed courtship, we were sitting in my apartment reading the paper when Ernest turned to the jewelry section and asked me,

"Which ring do you like?" in a general sort of way.

"Which ring do you want me to have?" was my serious response.

Somewhat stunned by my directness, he said, "Uh, let's go to Hudson's tomorrow."

I married this handsome man, Ernest Lee Travis, December 18, 1967, in Detroit, Michigan. The ceremony was performed by one of my father's colleagues. A few days later we went to Greensboro both to celebrate Christmas and to attend a wedding reception that my parents had planned for us.

Our reception was a beautiful southern reception. My father surprised me with a canopy that went from our front door down the walkway to the sidewalk. When I was much younger, I had said to my father that when I get married, I wanted a canopy to go from the door to the sidewalk. I could scarcely believe that he remembered, but this was just like him to take care of long standing promises.

The preparation for the reception, however, was not without a flaw. You guessed correctly if you thought that the flaw was caused by my Mother. She was attempting to make their spacious home as lovely and as accommodating as she could by removing some of the living room furniture for the receiving line. In doing so, she had removed my favorite chair. While she was running an errand, I brought the chair back into the room. A heated discussion ensued and Mother slapped me across my face on the day of my reception.

My father intervened and reprimanded my Mother for hitting me.

Hurt and embarrassed I retreated to my bedroom. Ernest came in to console me, but I would have no part of it.

"Why didn't you come to my defense?" I asked Ernest.

"Are you kidding? She looked like she would have hit me, too," was his response.

He wasn't too far from being right. Mother would not back down for anyone.

Perhaps, I owe the spunk that I had with the State Patrol to my mother.

After our marriage, Ernest and I began a prosperous life together in Detroit. He embraced my family and endeared himself to them. He pursued his education in a community college and began working on his Associate Degree. Lois Harris was instrumental in getting him to join my church. We truly became one happy and prosperous couple.

Ernest and I were opposites. He saved; I spent. He was a man of few words; I talked all of the time. Ernest was kind, thoughtful, and soon, very soon, all of my unpleasant previous memories of my bad marriage were in my past.

He did, however, on one occasion when I had irritated him say, "You know I don't fuss. I fight." A little bit of his previous street talk was manifesting itself.

Oh, brother, why did he say that. "Well, I don't know who you're going to fight because if you even as much play 'tag' with me and say, 'You're it!' I am gone forever." was my emphatic, resolute response.

There will never be another Jack. No more abuse for me! I still had that old gun.

That, nor anything similar, was ever said to me by Ernest again. Case closed.

In the eight years of our marriage, we bought two houses, one being in an exclusive suburb of Detroit, traveled to Hawaii, Mexico and Puerto Rico, enjoyed a nice lifestyle and both remained gainfully employed. Ernest readily embraced my values and my lifestyle and took my parents as his very own.

When we were in Greensboro for my father's annual convention, he would chauffeur my father to his appointments. My father would ask agreement from his jurisdictional pastors for Ernest to sit in on his business meetings.

Ernest observed and greatly admired my father's administrative style. For a class assignment he wrote an essay on, *What I Admire about My Father-in-Law.*

HERE I GO AGAIN

It seems that I could buckle up this time and be a little more prepared for tragedy, but I was not.

It was January 6, 1976, Ernest had celebrated his forty-sixth birthday on December 7th after we had just celebrated Christmas and New Years. My mother, who had just lost her husband, my father, had visited us. At last, the family was attempting to observe a normal holiday. Daddy's death had surprised and devastated us. This was the first holiday full of laughter, eating and visiting. Mother and I even took a quick bus trip to Benton Harbor, Michigan, to visit relatives and to attend New Years Eve service at my uncle's church. Ernest did not accompany us because he wanted to rest before returning to work.

It soon became time for mother to return to North Carolina, and I took her to the airport. I was somewhat disappointed because Ernest, who showed her, and my entire family, much affection, had not called to say, "Goodbye"

He later said that he had eaten something at work and did not feel well. Later, before retiring, he began rubbing his chest and saying that he was not feeling well. I immediately drove him to the hospital emergency room and he was given an examination. The attending physician determined that he had indigestion and a generic medicine was prescribed. The physician said that he could keep a normal schedule and the medicine would bring him relief. I insisted on his staying home the next day, but he refused. He had not missed a day of work in the eight years of our marriage.

Ernest seemed to have fully recovered and went ice skating on the nearby lake the next evening at dusk.

Twenty-four hours later, January 6, 1976, I got up to prepare to go to school and saw that Ernest was not in the bed. While going to the master bathroom, I saw that the light was on and that the door was open in the main bathroom. Both of us had a bad habit of not closing the bathroom door, so I called out to him, "Ernest, close the door."

There was silence.

I put on my bath robe and walked to the main bathroom and Ernest was face down in front of the commode on the floor. When I approached him, it was apparent that he was dead!!! Forty-six years old three weeks, and he was lying face down on the bathroom floor dead. Oh, my God!

I thought that I had experienced grief earlier when my beloved father had passed, but this one would later put her in almost an abyss of grief. I screamed and screamed until my larynx seemed to collapse and the noise turned into inaudible sobs. My neighbor heard me with her windows closed. My sister heard me when she began lifting the telephone off the receiver. How could this happen to me again so soon? Why? Why? Oh, God, where are you? Ernest is dead! Ernest dead! Was all that I could repeat as I frantically made calls to my neighbor, relatives and a few very close friends.

I would immediately hang up leaving them perplexed and having them to call a mutual friend and ask, "Did you just get a call from Claudia?"

"Yes. She screamed something that sounded like Ernest is dead. That can't be true. I'll call you back."

So the calls would come and I would pick up the telephone and immediately say again, "Ernest is dead. I just found him on the bathroom floor." I would hang up. I did not want to answer any questions.

Even the arrival of the officer from the West Bloomfield Police Department could not get a coherent response from me. Prior to the Officer's arrival, my neighbor, an anesthetist, went up to the bathroom to ascertain my belief. "Yes", she concurred, "Ernest is deceased." Rigor mortis had already set in.

The Officer added that he appeared to have been dead all night or at least for several hours, and that there must be a preliminary investigation and an autopsy to determine the cause and manner of his death. Was I to blame, I asked myself.

How can I forgive myself for sleeping while my husband was lying dead on the floor? Maybe, if I had not been so sound asleep, I could have saved him. What have I done?

"Call the Saints." I said repeatedly to the neighbor. Not understanding this terminology she said, "I don't see 'saints' listed in your telephone book."

"Lois Harris, that's her name." was my quick response.

I took to my bed and slept until the day of the funeral. There were no visitors, meals or coaxing that could get me out of the bedroom. I just wanted to be alone in my misery and grief.

The family and friends from North Carolina, Washington, Pennsylvania, New York, California and Virginia gathered to pay tribute to this kind man.

A beautiful memorial service was held in Detroit with hundreds in attendance. There was a great outpouring of love by clergy, family, professional colleagues, church members and friends. We flew to Greensboro, immediately after the memorial, to lay Ernest to rest beside my father. He had said earlier that he would like to be buried where my father was buried. I never uttered a single word during the entire flight from Detroit to Greensboro.

The family hour in Greensboro was too much and this grieving widow could not remain in the church for the entire allotted time. I left my friends and family in the church and went to my mother's condominium. DeOla, my strength in times of trouble, closed the bier.

We laid my husband to rest two graves from my father near a fountain and a large tree. That was a sad day. There was no comfort for me in a song or a card. I could not pray. When I got on my knees, a groan would come out. I again took to the bed in my mother's home.

Meanwhile, my mother and sister had to leave me immediately to attend my paternal uncle's funeral in Philadelphia.

Toney Mooney, my niece's future husband, who had never met me, stayed with me. They say that they die in threes, well, this was our third.

One afternoon, a group of saints came to the house to see me. I was lying across the bed with the bedspread over my head. When they came into the room, I acknowledged their presence, but I could not find the strength to remove the cover from over my head. I wanted to, but I could not. I finally apologized and told them that I would come out from under the covers and talk to them if they could return the next day. They sat in the room about forty-five minutes, prayed and left me under the bedspread covered up.

When I returned home to Michigan, there was never a time that I was left alone. Friends, Mabel Higgs spent the nights; Annabelle "Chick" Thomas did minor household chores, Zinnette and Rawleigh Lamb, Willie Mae Sheard, Ella Gordon, Barbara Benford, Delores Calhoun, and Ann Claudia Smith did everything that was possible to comfort me. When Ann Smith learned that I had a taste for a pound cake, she made me one, and drove over twenty miles late at night to bring it to me. My friends, especially Willie Mae Sheard, daily attended to me. Ella Gordon, Pierre and Rosalyn Merriwether stayed with me on weekends and encouraged me to go on with my life. I shall always love them.

Determined to be a lifelong widow, I dressed in black almost daily. The grief transcended into everything that I did. I once told my mother that I did not have a single smile left in me. The song, *I'll Never Smile Again* could be transposed to my permanent theme song.

When the choir director sent someone to ask me if I had a special request for them to sing during Sunday morning service, I replied, "Yes, sing, *Somebody's Done Somebody Wrong Song*. I refused to be comforted.

(left to right) Bishop Wells, Ernest Lee Travis, Claudia Travis, Mrs. Mary Wells

THERE IS A BRIGHT SIDE SOMEWHERE

On March 26, 1977, my principal summoned me to his office.

"Mrs. Travis, I have some bad news for you. Personnel called and said that we don't have enough white teachers on our staff for racial balance. So you will need to release the last black teacher that you received in your department for this new, white teacher," the principal said.

"Oh, my goodness! One of my best teachers is my most recently assigned black teacher. She is so good and the students and I both love her," was my immediate response.

"Ain't nothing that I can do. I am mad as hell! This teacher's present principal says that he is a racist and doesn't half come to school," he added.

I grunted. Did I not have enough problems, including the problems with the principal? Now, I was getting an incompetent racist. This is really going to disrupt and upset my academic program, I thought as I sat resolutely in the chair in the principal's office. "Okay. Thanks."

I left the office and began the dreaded adjustment process.

The next day, I went to the main office to await the arrival of this new racial balancer, Mr. Edmond Scott Hamilton.

Even though his car was stolen the night before, I later learned, Mr. Hamilton reported to the main office promptly. At least he was dependable and on time today. It was immediately evident that neither of us shared the pleasure professionally expected at this initial meeting.

I was thoroughly disgusted. A year later, when we discussed this initial meeting, I learned that he had looked at me and immediately thought, what in the world is all of that green stuff on her eyes. You see, my late husband, Ernest, had told me that green eye shadow was enhancing to a black lady. That morning, I had added a little extra for some unknown reason. Only God knows.

I introduced the teacher to her replacement. She was a jewel. Seeing my evident displeasure, when Mr. Hamilton walked away to his newly assigned mail box she quietly discreetly whispered, "Mrs. Travis, he's kinda handsome."

"Uh-huh." I grunted. I did not even pay him that much attention.

Within a year, my resilience must have unconsciously kicked in as I returned to a normal life. Trouble really should not last always. I had planned to cry every day for my beloved Ernest, but some days, I would forget. I would find myself laughing about something that I saw or heard. At first I would feel guilty of being happy, Nevertheless, laughter became more frequent. In fact, I stopped wearing black everyday and added a little pastel to my wardrobe. Consequently, within a year, I began going on dates with Edmond Hamilton, the new teacher. We have different versions of how this happened. We both agree that he pursued me; we differ on his tactics.

Edmond and I dated for ten years. Those years were both wonderful and tumultuous. We frequently argued, mainly about politics, as it appeared to me that he was a conservative; I, a liberal. One thing that bothered me and really angered me was his lack of admiration for some of the persons in the forefront of the civil rights movement, our heroes.

Secondly, in his conversations he often referred to my family, friends and me as exceptional in our life styles and accomplishments. I classified this as being stereotyped.

On the other hand, I had never met such a thoughtful, loving man. He was handy around my home and saw to it that repairs were made as needed. He seemed to always perceive my needs and proceeded to fulfill them. Additionally, he loved archeology, traveling and being in touch with nature. Yet, he did not seem annoyed by my love for exclusive apparel shopping, frequent charismatic church services, and utter disdain for outdoor activities. If opposites attract, we were a perfect example.

We were often challenged as an interracial couple when we were in public. In restaurants the hostesses seemed to have difficulty accepting the number in our party. After saying, two, we were also asked," Are the two of you together?" I wanted to say, "No, he just has his arm around my waist. The person that he is with is somewhere in the restaurant." Occasionally, they would seat us away from the other patrons under the pretense that they were providing us privacy. On one occasion when this remarked was made by a hostess, I replied, "Had we wanted privacy, we would have stayed home."

I also had some fun with one person who exhibited prejudices. Once in a theater in an exclusive suburb, an elderly Caucasian man, who was with a lady that I assumed to be his wife, stared at me with utter disdain. I looked, smiled and said to him loudly with familiarity, "Hi. Ed, look who is here," I further said, directed to the man," I did not know that you lived out here."

He quickly looked away, and his wife turned and looked at him as if to ask, "Do you know her?"

Ed and I exited out of the theater as if we had seen an acquaintance. I later said outside, "I bet he regrets that dirty look that he gave to me. He might have some explaining to do."

Because we were very much in love, we were able to resolve all issues amicably. One evening at a restaurant, Ed unexpectedly proposed to me and I immediately said, "Yes."

We immediately went to my Mother's home, awakened her, and I happily exclaimed, ""Mother, Ed just proposed to me, and I said yes."

She rubbed her eyes, sat up in the bed and said, "It's about time."

It must have been divine intervention that sent Edmond to integrate the school, and to be in my department and my life. After dating for ten years, and making some necessary, major adjustments for an interracial relationship, on November 28, 1987, we exchanged vows, and I became Mrs. Edmond Scott Hamilton. Approximately one hundred family members and friends witnessed our exchange of vows in a beautiful, new local palatial hotel.

As I reflect on my marriages, all three were a bit out of the ordinary.

My first marriage was a man who was very much my senior. In fact, my mother and he were born on the same day and the same year. My second marriage was plagued by the stigma of my husband's occupation as a cosmetologist. My third marriage is interracial.

It seems evident that my proclivity is for challenges. even in my romantic relationships. I must reiterate that I do welcome challenges.

After twenty-five years of marital bliss, I have found Edmond to be the kindest, supportive and most loving husband for which I could ever hope. I hope to spend the rest of my life with him. He tells me every day that he loves me, and I truly love him with all of my heart.

I truly learned that here is a bright side on the other side of the storm. Don't rest until you find it.

Mr. and Mrs. Edmond Scott Hamilton

SEEING THE WORLD PERSONALLY

Our passports have not stayed tucked safely away for any length of time since Ed and I began our ten year courtship and marriage. Meeting Ed opened up a new traveling experience vista for me.

Before meeting Ed my previous travels had been limited to Hawai, Mexico City, Acapulco, San Juan and Toronto. Personally, I believe that if God has an earthly home, it is in Hawaii. Also, my world before meeting Ed was mainly North Carolina and the eastern coast of the United States of America.

Every summer, beginning with 1983, Ed and I would pull out our passports and fly to Europe, which included Germany, Copenhagen, Switzerland, the Netherlands, Austria, Italy, France, Norway, Spain and Sweden. We would go as far as his money would take us, which also included Montego Bay, Puerto Rico, Montreal and Vancouver.

We have seen nature and its splendor, enjoyed native cuisine, seen the ruins of the world; prayed and had communion in great Cathedrals. We have prayed in the Sistine Chapel in Rome. We have viewed the ruins of Rome; sat on the Spanish Steps. We have watched the changing of the guards in London many times. We have traveled the autobahn through the various landscapes and viewed the mystic Black Forest and majestic mountains. We have motored west in the United States and visited the mesas of the native Indians, the Grand Canyon, the Hoover Dam, and the coastal highways of California. We have enjoyed the excitement and glitz of Las Vegas, Reno and Lake Tahoe. We have followed the banks of the majestic Colorado River. We have experienced the leisure life of Sausalito, Montego Bay, Hollywood, Los Angeles and the trolley of San Francisco.

We shall never forget our visit by train to the French Rivera in Nice. I can vividly recall the roar of the car motors as they speeded down the avenues, the craggy, oily banks of the Mediterranean Sea with their topless women basking in the sunshine, the busy smoke- filled casinos with the elite gamblers. I tried my luck with the one armed bandits, got lucky, and immediately left, while I was ahead. I was awed by the splendor and elegantly dressed patrons and the plush, decadence of the Monte Carlo casinos.

God's world and its splendor have unfolded before our eyes as we observed varying local scenic landscapes, terrains, majestic mountains of Utah and Colorado. There were times when it seemed to me that God was saying, "Look, Claudia, can you describe this?" to which my response would have to be, "How great Thou art!"

Edmond and I have resided in plush hotels in Singapore, Bangkok and Hong Kong. We have weathered the Mon Soon rains. We have had the service of a personal butler and on site room registration. We have dined on five course meals in five star hotels. We have toured cities in limousines. We have taken advantage of the mercantile that traveling provides and worn garments made by their skillful hands. Ed has enabled me the experience of wearing Chanel garments, the finest.

I have organized and escorted ten women from Michigan on a shopping trip for seven days to Paris, France. We visited the Louvre and Versailles and tasted the finest pastries and French cuisine. We have walked the Champs Elysees, climbed the Eiffel Towers viewed the Arc de Triumph, and enjoyed native holiday celebrations.

We have experienced a 20/20 vision of a goodly portion of God's beautiful world.

Our travels had been generally without a negative event because we were warned by travel agencies to be alert and not to be obvious tourists. Our trips, for the most part were without incident. Sadly, it troubles me to recall that I was pick-pocketed in 2011 of Fourteen Hundred dollars in Hong Kong during their New Years celebration. I did learn a great spiritual lesson from that loss, so there was some gain in the experience.

Most of the time, we disguised our cameras under our wraps and made our video cameras as inconspicuous as possible. We avoided that tourist look.

However, a humorous incident in Amsterdam readily comes to mind. One day we became engrossed in discovering Ann Frank's hideout and looking at the interesting blocks of sidewalk graffiti and began to let our guard down. In the nick of time, I noticed a man and woman eyeing us and separately easing closer to us.

They were startled when just as they were positioning to perhaps grab our bags, I said, in a threatening voice, "Come on. I am from Detroit."

They stopped in their tracks and quickly departed. Ed, until this day, is amused to recall this incident and the look of surprise on their faces.

We, with our Detroit savvy, avoided Ed being pick-pocketed in the Nord Terminal of the airport in Paris, France. We found that being from notorious Detroit is a vital reminder when traveling in Europe. A stoop, drop theft was roughly avoided by us on the escalator. Our luggage became weapons. They had no idea that Ed and I were together, so we teamed up on them and caught them by surprise. I watch and pray, sometimes one more than the other.

East Berlin was dismal and in vast contrast to West Berlin. We cherish fond memories of our days in bustling West Berlin. It reminded us of the cosmopolitan spirit of New York. A movie was being made in our hotel during our visit which heightened the ambience. Also, we visited the popular zoo of West Berlin.

We recall, with consternation, the tumultuous night on the high North Sea, after traveling all day on a sooty train ride without air condition. I was so disheveled and sweaty that I tried to pretend that I was not with Ed. The sea was restless, the tide was high and spilling water over the lower deck. Mt. Union kept coming back to mind, so I took a Vicodin and slipped into La-la Land for the remainder of the voyage. Ed kept a vigilant watch over me to protect me from the possible knaves. Ed is always there and ready to protect me.

When we embarked, Ed rented me a shower stall, in Gothenburg, before we proceeded on to see my granddaughter, Emma, in the village of Haalmsted, Sweden.

I had never been to London before 1987. In fact, it shames me now to recall how authoritative I was in telling why London was not a good place for tourists. My account, from hearsay was that it was foggy, rainy and that the food was simply horrible.

My sister, who was the only person in which Ed had confided, knew our honeymoon destination. My sister told me to pack clothes for a cold climate. Months earlier we had renewed our passports My curiosity ran the gamut. Two days after our wedding and the departure of out of state guests, Ed told me to be prepared to leave immediately for our honeymoon. We said goodbye and got in the car. A few minutes afterward, Edmond said, "We are driving to Toronto to board a non-stop flight to London, England."

Our honeymoon was the source of the beginning of my love for London. To date, we have returned six times for a week or more "holiday." A girl can spend days or lose her mind in Harrods' or Selfridge's Department Stores. They have hats galore and clothes to make a shopper spend her last pound or shilling.

A trip to London, England, has also been our graduation gift to three of our grandchildren, Jason, Chandra and Emma. Jason was the only one who seemed really impressed. The girls just said, "It's okay."

Our love for London is only rivaled by our love and return to Bangkok and Hong Kong. We seldom, to date, miss two years without making our annual trek to Hong Kong. Frankly, I am attracted by not only the culture, but also the landscape and the food. Tailoring and the designing of a lot of my special wardrobe garments are made in Hong Kong and Bangkok. A designer suit can be measured, fitted and completed in one day. Their sewing skills are impeccable.

Oh, by the way, before I forget, the new teacher was right! I concur wholeheartedly with her opinion of Mr. Hamilton's looks.

IF I CAN HELP SOMEBODY, MY LIVING IS NOT IN VAIN

Those years in North Carolina and Detroit Public Schools were well spent. Remember that my goal was to have a positive impact on the lives of young people. During my tenure, I attempted to teach, nurture, support, encourage, feed, protect and to set a Christian example to those with whom I came in contact. Frequently, when I am in some public place, I am reunited with a former student who expresses gratitude for something that I did for them. One former student from North Carolina, Sandra Watts Wallace, has sent me a Christmas card every year since 1959. Clifford Parker, a student since 1980, calls me every Christmas and Mother's Day. Lela Fullerton, 1980, visits me annually. Several former secretaries, staff and teachers stay in touch with me with a card, visit or telephone call.

It was not just the young people that I wanted to touch. I also tried to help the adults under my supervision or with whom I am contact. Several adults were encouraged to pursue a degree and or to purchase a home. My personal secretary, with my persistent urging, has earned her bachelor and masters degrees. Presently, she is pursuing her doctorate degree. Personal scholarships and monetary assistance have been given by me and/or my husband almost yearly. Nothing makes me happier than meeting someone else's need.

Oh, I have had some nicknames like, Hard Hearted Hannah or other terms not necessarily of endearment, some earned; some not. I do know that in my heart that there was not any malice towards anyone. I just did my job and loved every minute of it. It's alright to be hard on the outside, but I must be sweet on the inside.

FACTORING IN THE FAITH

Since accepting Christ as my personal Savior at an early age, I have learned to believe that faith could remove any obstacle that one faced. In fact, opportunity to exemplify strong faith is welcomed. I often remind others that there are no impossibilities when one operates under the premise that no matter how it seems, God can and will do exactly what He said that He would do. Time, however, taught me that God worked on His own time and deadlines, and that faith must be coupled with patience and submission to God's will.

Perhaps, my strong belief in the power of faith also enabled me to always seek a solution to any problem with which I was faced. Sometimes, a simple no will inspire me and set me in a determination mode to have the no changed to yes. For an example, if I am seeking to purchase something and the clerk casually says, "We are out of…" I will insist on the clerk's looking again for the item. I can't tell you the times when this last minute search produced the item. My persistence occasionally becomes an annoyance, but I have many times had a "I can't" changed to, "Okay, just this one time."

Deep down in my heart, I believe that good things will not be withheld from me, if I seek God first.

When I became a principal in a high needs urban public high school, I almost daily practiced lots of faith, while getting the somewhat impossible done. Remember that I was shaped to be nice and friendly and I practiced this in my business dealings. Even though I always remain professional, I always responded to my supervisors and peers in a very friendly, warm manner. Occasionally, I would get a response like, "Do I know you?" during a telephone conversation. Consequently, I was able, with the assistance of many of the school board members and superintendents, to get repairs, program and services that had previously been denied to my predecessors. The school, where I was principal, was later designated as one of the most advanced school of technology in the local school system. I believe that my prayers and faith that this school would make a vast improvement is still being answered, even after my retirement.

Faith brings about persistence; persistence frequently results in success. The scripture says,

> I can do all things through Christ which strengtheneth me.
>
> Philippians 4:13 (KJV)

Yes, this includes moving obstacles that thwart growth, progress and success. With faith you can experience victory.

YOU CAN'T WIN THEM ALL

You can't win them all, but you can certainly show up for the audition.

It was necessary for me to learn that even those who have faith will possibly sometime not have their projected outcome. I have come to believe that losing, teaches as good a lesson, as well as winning does. The victories possibly fall short of the lessons learned from losing. Maybe, just maybe, losing can be a victory.

In fact, I can't recall many of my victories, but the memories of the losses linger and sting. One experience lingers.

I applied for a position as principal in a prestigious high school in another school district. I was recommended for the position by a former colleague. The offer came at an opportune time in my career and offered both professional and monetary benefits. In my present position as an assistant principal there were some politics favoring certain staff. My position precluded the advancement of this staff, and an effort was made to discredit my performance standards to promote her to my position.

The interview for the new position went well, I thought. My background in drama helped me in my responses to questions asked. I had learned to look into the eyes of whomever was interviewing and respond with authority. There was one question posed to me that caused me some consternation:

"Mrs, Hamilton, what do you think about Tracking?" the interviewer asked.

For the love of me, even though the special education teacher spoke occasionally about it, I could not recall what "Tracking" was. "Well", I composed myself and said with authority, "I thoroughly believe that sometimes tracking is effective, on the other hand, I believe that sometimes tracking is harmful."

There was silence. I looked directly at the interviewer, after my profound answer.

Notwithstanding this ambiguous response, the interview ended well. I was told, off of the record, that my interview was excellent, and that I would be notified of their decision on the following Monday. I was further confidentially informed that the appointment of the position was between another principal and me, with the possibility of my being the favorite.

I left elated.

In the meantime, the next day after returning from the interview, Personnel called me and told me that I had been promoted to principal of a local high risk school that had been without a principal for a year. I was further instructed that I was to report to the new assignment the next day. Unbelievable! What was the urgency now?

Knowing that the decision was to be made in a day or two for the new position, I requested that my promotion be delayed a day or two to give me time for closure at my present job. I really wanted to stall or delay the appointment for obvious reasons. The request was denied and the compromise was for me to report to my new assignment a day later, the same day that the selection committee was to notify me of their decision.

Adversity never takes a holiday. Adversity precluded my being assigned to the position. The Selection Committee expressed an unwillingness to get involved in what seemed to be an unusual political situation. Their presence indicated that I had previously been selected. I felt so defeated until I did not have the professional energy to present my preference or my case. This was one time when I should have expressed myself.

This situation really hurt me deeply and made me bitter. I believed that a personal vendetta, by a person who shall remain unidentified, had precluded my appointment to principal of this prestigious school. My private thoughts reduced me to my lowest denominator. I wanted revenge.

When I expressed the fact that I wanted to get revenge to an administrator for what he had done to me, my confidant and Edmond scolded me and expressed alarm and disappointment that I could verbalize such an evil thought. Could this have been a crumbling process?

In the days that followed, I sought, but could not find comfort.

It was my son, Thaddeus, who shook me into the reality of the rational way to accept a loss.

"Mother," he said. "How many finalists were there for the position?"

"Two."

"Well, did it not dawn on you that both of you couldn't be appointed?"

I was silent.

He continued, "Did it not dawn on you that you could win or lose? If so, why are you so surprised that you lost? If you were as smart as I believe you to be, you would have considered both options."

My son was right. How could I not entertain the thought of losing? It is easy to win, but it takes class to lose graciously. Case is closed. Hold your head up high and be somebody!

Healing slowly began. There was so much needed, and I went on to stir up another pitcher of lemonade at Southeastern High School. "A Rose in the Dessert," became our new slogan displayed in the main hall.

The building located in a deprived neighborhood was drab and in much need of renovations. The purple front entrance door was their main source of pride. One thing the students and community had was personal pride of their less than adequate surroundings. It was a badge of honor to say that you were from the East Side. The Jungaleers was their mascot even though no one could describe a "jungaleer'. The students, on the other hand, were very disruptive, truant and the atmosphere not conducive to learning. The school and the staff needed direction and leadership.

The staff was competent, but not inspired to perform to their highest levels of competency.

On my second day, a parent came to enroll her son in school. She preference our conference by telling me how much she dreaded the enrollment because of the appearance and the reputation of the school.

I cannot tell you why, but I immediately got up from my desk, went to the inter-communication system and asked the students for their attention.

"May I have your attention, please. This is Mrs. Hamilton, your new principal. I have a parent in my office enrolling her son. This parent just informed me that she hates enrolling her son here because she feels that the school is dirty, ugly and the students are bad. I am returning to my desk to tell her that with your help, we can make this school a rose in the dessert, and that each of you will sign a pledge that I shall have circulated on tomorrow stating that you are willing to make self-improvement. If you agree, say, 'Yes' right now. Pause. I can hear your responses from the rooms. Remember that a rose can survive in a dessert if it is watered daily. Our good behavior can water the rose. Thank you for your attention. Goodbye."

When I returned to my desk, the parent seemed stunned. "Wow, you are something else." she said. The State Patrol first said that in different words.

I smiled very politely, "Yes, I have been told that I am a bit unusual."

Thus, Southeastern High School became known as The Rose in the Dessert.

The changes were rapid. I offered prizes for beautifying classroom doors; had all of the halls painted; placed incentive ceiling flags in the main corridor; refurbished the lobby and dedicated the portraits of administrators, past and present; repaired the sports trophy showcase, furnished and air conditioned the teachers' lounge\; bought furniture for the conference room and air conditioned it; refurbished the main office and furnished my personal office state of the art with my personal funds. Southeastern High School took on a new slogan and a new look. This was culminated with an elaborate catered Open House and Unveiling Ceremony of former and present principals for school personnel and the community. The school took on a new look and drastic change in atmosphere and academic climate.

Academically, a proposal was written by selected staff members and the school was selected and entered into a compact. My colleagues ridiculed me for selecting to compact with the Internal Revenue Service, rather than a company that could and would provide monetary funds. I felt that my students needed tutorial, remedial service in reading, mathematics and science. Contrary to popular belief, things can not improve the mind. Employees of The Internal Revenue volunteered to give me forty-eight hours worth of tutorial service per week. It worked! My test scores and stanines improved in the selected areas, and Southeastern showed vast improvement, thus, getting the attention of Chrysler Motors. Chrysler later adopted Southeastern High School, and donated a million dollars for its physical improvement. Today, it stands as a citadel for the Detroit Public High Schools.

Even though I was given the choice to enroll my grandson, Jason, in one of the more highly regarded schools, I chose to enroll my grandson into Southeastern. This personal example prompted other faculty members to enroll their children. Teachers were being more closely monitored because students discuss, at the dinner table, what goes on in the classroom. The instruction was greatly improved as reflected by their Performance Standard Reviews, and teachers were rewarded with certificates, plaques and luncheons. The school climate became optimistic and bright.

Southeastern High School, with the help of many, truly became "A Rose in the Dessert".

I remained happily on this challenging assignment until my retirement in 1994. The loss of the other prestigious appointment was, indeed, a victory.

THE ULTIMATE PERSONAL TEST

During the last of June, 2000, my greatest test of faith would come in Wilson, North Carolina, a beautiful, southern town in eastern North Carolina where I had had that encounter with the State Patrol forty years earlier.

A few hours before departing West Bloomfield, Michigan, on our much needed vacation, I took my second bath for the night before retiring for a few hours sleep. I had taken one earlier bath, but some last minute chores caused me to perspire and have the need to refresh myself. Just as I had done earlier, I examined my breasts. I discovered a large lump in my right breast. This came as a surprise because it was my daily practice to examine my breasts. It was very difficult for me to accept what I was feeling. I had never expected an examination to reveal any abnormalities. This examination was just an intelligent routine that women were advised to take.

The fourth of July was within a few days and my husband, Edmond, and I decided that it would be next to impossible to see a local physician without an earlier appointment. In addition, I had just selected a new primary care physician that I had never met. So, we decided to proceed with our vacation plans, and I promised him faithfully that I would make a serious attempt to see a physician when we reached our destination, Wilson, North Carolina. The possibility of it being a benign cyst was also discussed. We certainly did not want to create a false crisis.

Hours after our arrival, I informed my hostess of my discovery. It was hard for me to say that I had a lump in my breast. She began right away trying to get an appointment for a mammogram. She, too, was persistent, and I shall never forget Inez Bell for the take charge attitude that she showed in getting me to a clinic within an hour or so.

The personnel at the Wilson Clinic greeted me warmly with their southern hospitality. Nevertheless, all of the warmth in Phoenix could not lighten the shock of hearing, "We believe that the spot that you see on the screen is malignant. Also, we see some discoloration of the lymph nodes indicating that some of them may be involved."

Boom! Boom! I have been hit with a time bomb. I have cancer!

In every previous situation in my life, I was on the outside of the situation. Everything traumatic that had happened in my life involved another party or outside sources. My abuse, my grief had both come from my reaction or what I was allowing someone to do to me or what was happening outside of me. This was totally different. My health was the situation.

I could not choose not to take it personally or to accept or to reject it. It was personal. **I** have cancer! It is in my body. My body is the source of my distress. I did not put the lump in; I cannot take it out. It is there and growing on its own.

The cookie crumbled momentarily.

Silently, almost reverently, I stood holding my husband's hand. I turned, looked at him and asked the only question that came to mind, "Ed, will you still love me?" I had seen cancer patients who looked gaunt and dissipated and that's how I envisioned myself. This question embarrassed my husband and the physician. My husband assured me that he would never stop loving me, and the physician concurred that he would probably love me more.

There was nothing for me to say. I was going to die. I felt that I was facing death, and I stood there holding my husband's hand. The news had stunned me, even though I was fully aware of the pros and the cons of the situation in which I found myself. There was little else for me to say. I felt that I was facing an inevitable death, and that I stood silently before God and His mercy. I must hold my head up high and be somebody, even when facing death.

The old Negro Spiritual goes, "I know the Lord. I know the Lord, I know the Lord has His hands on me."

Within a few days, the fear of death completely left me. I was in the hands of a loving God, and I would be taken care of. All that I needed to do is not waver and stand strong.

The scripture says,

> Wherefore take unto you the whole armour of God, that ye may be able to withstand in the evil day, and having done all, to stand. Stand.
>
> Ephesians 6:13 (KJV)

There is blessed assurance when one believes that he is in God's hands. I did believe, for my comfort and sanity.

Knowing and trusting in God do not exempt one from the realities of life, and I believe that suffering is a necessary experience for growth. There are, however, basic truths that must be remembered. First, that there is not a storm that God can't dispel; secondly, the more fierce the storm, the shorter the duration. Perhaps, this conclusion could be challenged, but in the scheme of things, the eye of a storm comes quickly and passes quickly. It is the anticipation and the aftermath that makes the storm seem lengthy. Our attitude determines the duration of the aftermath.

After the dreadful news, we continued on our planned itinerary to go to Maine.

A brief visit with my goddaughter, Adrienne, and her new husband in Fort Washington, Pennsylvania, was our next stop. In route, a call had been made to a dear friend, Marilyn Robinson, asking her to contact and to set up an appointment for me with my new primary care physician. After arriving at my goddaughter's palatial home, little was said about the diagnosis. Every attempt was made to make the Fourth of July holiday a happy day. Other guests from Africa dominated interesting and diverse conversations. Everything went well. Our hostess and host, Adrienne and P.J., created a festive mood. They cooked loads of food, fried a turkey, and I ate like I was starved.

I had promised a dear friend, LeVonia Whittley, from Chicago that I would come to Houston, Texas, to introduce her before she delivered her annual AIMS Convention address. I boarded the plane in Philadelphia, left my husband behind, and flew to Houston, Texas. All the while, all I could think of was, that I have cancer. In the terminal, I would look at people and think, they have no idea that that they are looking at maybe a dying lady. I would have an occasional relapse of optimism.

Upon my arrival in Houston, I joined my friends and my brother who were attending the convention. I made a feeble attempt to tell my cousin and a friend, but I alluded to the fact that something was wrong. Everyone seemed a bit uncomfortable, including my brother. So, I went to my lonely hotel room and looked over my introduction speech.

I was anxious to get out of that lonely room and arrived quite early for the service. Naturally, I was seated on the platform with the bishops, dignitaries and the officers of the national church with whom I had grown. It was difficult for me to keep my composure and to stay focus. My recent diagnosis preoccupied my thoughts.

The time came. I stood before the vast audience and delivered what I believe to have been a very dynamic and effective introduction. When I turned to return to my seat, the

Presiding Bishop, Bishop Chandler Owens, got up stopped me and said, "Claudia, you looked and sounded just like your Daddy standing there."

"Pray for me, Bishop Owens. I shall be with him soon," was my response.

He stared a bit perplexed at my response.

I was trembling as I reached my seat. I felt that I had just completed my farewell speech to the Saints. This could possibly be my last national convention.

I was seated beside my covenant sister, Pearl Hill, from Michigan. I turned to her and said, "Pearl, I have something to tell you. I have just been diagnosed with cancer."

She looked shocked. Before she could reply, I got up, left the platform to return to my room. I could not keep the masquerade as I went down the aisle. Ella Gordon saw my distress and accompanied me out of the auditorium, inquiring to know what was wrong. I made no attempt to answer her. I just thanked her for her concern and boarded the shuttle bus back to the hotel.

I got a large bath towel, put it over my mouth and screamed and screamed until I became almost hysterical. My brother calling me on the telephone to apologize for being unable to hear me give my introduction, timely interrupted my private pity party.

In the early dawn hours, I joined other delegates, my friends, Bishop and Mrs. Frank White, a couple from New York, to board a plane. I returned to Philadelphia. I could not, however continue the masquerade on our vacation to Maine.

I wanted to return home. So, Ed agreed to do so. He drove all night and returned to West Bloomfield, Michigan.

Telling my mother, sister and son was very difficult. Later, everyone was very optimistic and supportive. DeOla said, "The devil is a liar."

Mother was quiet.

Thaddeus sort of played it off with, "You'll be alright."

After additional routine tests and examinations, the surgeon and I decided that a lumpectomy would be the appropriate procedure for me to have. So, I underwent lumpectomy surgery on July 31, 2000.

After my lumpectomy, I began comforting myself through verse. I wrote *God Has Got His* Hands *on Me* and gave every visitor to my room a copy. Secondly, I decided on a theme song, *Jesus Never Fails,* best expressed my sentiments. So, even though some visitors were reluctant or tearful, I would ask each visitor to join me in singing, my song, and I would sing as a solo the last verse that says, "I've tried Him, He never fails."

Mother Willie Mae Rivers, the National Supervisor of Women for the Church of God in Christ, visited me in my bedroom, brought a beautiful plant and joined in the singing of, *Jesus Never Fails*, prayed and left. I was truly honored by her presence.

My spirit was dampened when thirty days after my lumpectomy, tests had revealed more cancer in my breast and lymph nodes. I underwent a mastectomy and the removal of two lymph nodes. I kept singing, *Jesus Never Fails*.

During the interval, as chairperson of the First Annual Crystal Scholarship Banquet, I presided over a scholarship banquet at the Hyatt Hotel one week after the lumpectomy. One thousand dollars each was awarded to eight deserving, young high school graduating scholars. Hundreds including my committee, my husband, my mother, son, niece and nephew, my grandson, goddaughter and my granddaughter proudly attended and supported me. In his closing remarks, the late Bishop Walter Emile Bogan, Sr., praised my leadership and compared me to an injured athlete who would get up and stay in the game after being sacked. I truly had been sacked.

I chaired two more Crystal Scholarship Banquets after the first one. I was instrumental in awarding thirty-three thousand dollars worth of scholarships to the young people in Great Lakes First Ecclesiastical Michigan Jurisdiction, with the help of a wonderful committee.

The evening later proved to be a medical challenge. Pearl Hill was there again and accompanied me to my hotel room to bathe my infected, unpleasant incision. She did it with such love and tenderness. This was a magnificent act of kindness on her part that will never be forgotten.

When you are being treated with chemotherapy, the treatment is usually lasts two hours. It is the sick feeling like rotten chickens were in my stomach, the nausea, the loss of energy, the loss of all hair, the black finger and toe nails, the loss of taste buds, and the loss of appetite that make the suffering feel endless. It takes real effort not to get despondent.

On many occasions, eating became a dreaded chore. My mouth broke out in sores, thrash. So, I would not eat, and the body functions became affected. The taste buds could not distinguish a steak from gelatin All food had identical bitter tastes. Strawberry and cherry popsicles became my substitute for carbohydrates, proteins, minerals, iron and other daily dietary needs. This was the aftermath of the chemotherapy storm.

Potato salad is my most favorite food in the world. Occasionally, Wilda Newton or Rose Malenfant would make me some potato salad. I would eat that even though it also had a bitter taste. I just love potato salad! Mother Rosa Hawkins would also prepare me a meal. All were great cooks trying to help. Sadly, Newton and Hawkins died from cancer within a few years of my diagnosis.

Oddly enough, loss of hair had almost a positive effect on me. I have always enjoyed changing hair styles. I have even been known to change a flattering hairstyle for a less flattering. Loss of hair, during chemotherapy, is almost inevitable, so, I made preparation early on to cope, prior to the hair loss. My husband once remarked, "I think that Claudia is looking forward to being bald headed." Not so, it was just time to make a little lemonade and I needed to make preparations.

All of the major cosmetic companies were contacted. I explained my medical condition and the pending possibility of the loss of hair. I requested the cosmetic company to put me in touch with a local beauty consultant that could advise me as to how I could apply make up to enhance my black features with a bald head. Clinique was the only company that responded with some referrals.

To aid my mental adjustment, my sister and some of her friends in Memphis, Tennessee, gave me an earring party in my hotel room. They selected large earrings to accent my African features. I pretended to be an African queen. Hold your head up high and be somebody.

I never considered putting on a wig. What was I going to pin it to? I always wore hats. In fact, I have a hat closet with several hundred hats in it. However, when I wore a hat, the perspiration from my head would ruin the band and dissolve the glue. So, I just oiled my bald head, my husband would shave my head, and I went about my daily schedule. Often, women would approach me and say, "I like your shaven head. I wish I had the nerve to shave mine."

"God did it, and I have accepted it." was my usual response. This was just another glass of lemonade. I could have had a lemonade stand franchise by now

STRENGTH PERSONIFIED

My mother has always been the driving force in my life. It has always amazed me to observe the strength that she showed. Though rather small in stature, she had a giant of a spirit and determination to stand up fearlessly against any opposition and to somehow come out the victor. She was an only child and was accustomed to having her way and winning. Mother neither had a job growing up nor worked outside of the home. She was her own boss until she married my father. He, however, did not cherish that role.

Mother was very proud. My father would often remind her that the bible condemned being proud. This reminder never really fazed her, and she would give him that familiar look of disgust. For the sake of peace, even my strong father hesitated to challenge Mother.

It was generally known that mother lived by the rules of accepted social etiquette, proper behavior and her own rules.

Our home was a place where visitors were welcomed by my father. Mother would have always preferred that her home would be for her family exclusively, but my father's wishes prevailed in this matter. Ministers, who came to run a week or a two week revival would be guests in our home. Mother insisted on cleanliness and proper etiquette at the table. Later, it was said that ministers would refer to the visit as a week at Yale University.

In the 60's Mother had a maid. In fact, she had a maid for upstairs who cleaned upstairs and cooked the meals; a downstairs maid who attended to DeOla's two young preschool daughters, while she, her husband and children temporarily lived at home, and they cleaned the downstairs.

Dinner was served promptly at six o'clock and everyone was expected to be properly dressed and groomed. Each family member had his/her seat and my father presided at the head of the table. The table had to be set properly with napkins. No bottles or canned drinks were permitted to be on the table. A water pitcher was permitted and my father's glass must always be kept filled with water. He drank water throughout the meal. The meals, except for holidays, were served family style. On holidays, each dish was served individually. The only food on the table for the holiday meal would be a turkey, a ham or prime rib, the cranberry sauce, deviled eggs and other condiments. The second turkey and the second ham, for the holiday meal, were carved in the kitchen and served. The turkey and ham on the table were not carved and they were later frozen for a future meal.

Mother had endured hardships in her early days, but she was a strong woman and survived with great style and dignity. Mother stressed dignity. Hold your head up high and be somebody was her lifelong admonition. Additionally, she was always very stylish. It could possibly be said that she was a fashion trend setter in her church world.

The furniture capital of the United States is High Point, North Carolina. My father took advantage of the availability of discounted, elegant furniture and our home and its furnishings were well appointed and widely admired. People whispered that the Wellses are the Huxtables, referring to Bill Crosby's television family.

Needless to say, that I was greatly influenced by my Mother. Cleanliness, beauty, organization, fashion and proper etiquette have been infused in my lifestyle. Even though I preferred a disposition like my father, it appears that there is a greater resemblance to my mother in other aspects.

As Mother entered her late 80's, it became apparent that her health was failing. Even though she needed a lot of assistance, she would almost daily remind whoever was her caretaker that," I am not going to let you take me over." She continued to be resolute and of an independent spirit. Additionally, she kept a clear, lucid mind.

In Memphis, Tennessee, on the morning of July 21, 2005, at the age of 92, with DeOla by her bedside, Mother transcended into her new, eternal life. God stood by her and sustained her until He lovingly took her into His arms.

We laid her in her final resting place in Greensboro, North Carolina, beside of her beloved husband, near a water fountain and under a shady, oak tree.

My sadness was lessened by wonderful, happy and some-times humorous, fond memories. Thoughts of my Mother usually make me smile. When the family gets together, the conversations finally end with, "Remember when Mama…?" She was unique.

Needless to say, Mother greatly influenced my life and I'll always love and fondly remember her.

PREPARING FOR THE END OF MY JOURNEY

I have been blessed to celebrate my 83rd birthday and thoughts of going the last mile comes to mind frequently. While preparing, I want to stay busy working to do the will of the Lord and to continue to serve my fellowman, especially young people.

The encounters of life often thwart progress, yet they are necessary to complete the process. I do not shun adversity. In fact, I expressed earlier that I welcome adversity because it causes a flow of adrenalin that forces me into the action, aggressive mode.

Now, I often find myself sitting, thoughts drifting with lagging recall. The physical body, to which I owe every move that I have made, seems to not be as eager to respond to my commands. This alert mind that produced all of those creative, wonderful ideas, often becomes confused and unable to recall the simplest thing like my friends' name or where I ate last Sunday. I forget what I am going for; can't remember what

I was doing before I began going for something. My energy seems to be somewhere else. I seldom really hear what is said to me. After a few, "What did you say?", I pretend that I have heard. The weeks seem short; the days repetitious.

The world is scary; people are violent and mean. They don't just murder you, they dismember your body. It isn't as safe as it use to be. Children can't play hopscotch on the public sidewalk. Students don't memorize and recite, *Somebody's Mother* in school anymore. In fact, a young criminal said on the evening news that he targets the elderly to rob. The young people seem weaned from the milk of human kindness. Everybody has a gun, and personal ownership of a gun by each citizen has been mandated by a small town in Georgia. The Second Amendment seems to be the most important of all of the other amendments. The rest of the amendments and the Ten Commandments can be ignored. Even teachers might be permitted to bear arms in the classroom. It is not clear is it in God or in guns that America trusts?

My life has been built on religious tenets, and most especially I have accepted the principles of holiness. Practices of holy living and love for thy neighbor have been permitted to be compromised. It is difficult for me to accept the dogmas permitted and practiced in our homes, community, government and churches. The compromise seems to have eliminated high moral standards and regard for the welfare of our fellowman. Disputes are settled with guns; moral standards are adjusted according to demands. It's a new day! The game that my playmate introduced to me on her kitchen floor is acceptable by the adults in the bedroom and people of the same sex appear at the altar to make a lifetime commitment to this lifestyle. Will God bless America? Listen to the news.

Where can I turn for a definitive answer? To my church?

My church affiliations have been the source of my greatest joys and deepest wounds. Perhaps, my greatest regret, in this respect, is my church's hesitation, on the national level, to use my talents that they encouraged me to sharpen. I was told by the pioneers to get a good education. Yet, later, insecurities, lack of trust, and other inhibitors prevailed, making me unsuitable for appropriate appointments as they compared their knee education, prayer life, to my formal education, assuming that I could not have both. It has not been easy for me to watch people promoted or given responsibilities above their competency level, while a person of competency was overlooked or to watch neophytes promoted over persons with tenure and experience.

I understand, however, that, in the scheme of things, strength comes from endurance. There are no alternatives. In this respect the spiritual, religious, world and the secular world seem not to differ.

So, as I review my life and life's situation, it becomes a struggle to refrain from crumbling completely.

One of the lasting joys that can bring comfort as I get closer to the end of the journey is to love and to be loved. In that respect, it is with great thanks that I have the love of my husband, son, grandchildren, family and selected friends.

Oh, yes, I have a deep, abiding love for the Saints everywhere, especially the saints of Greater Love Tabernacle Church of God in Christ and Greater Emmanuel Institutional Church of God in Christ, Detroit, Michigan and Greater North Carolina Ecclesiastical Jurisdiction.

Time and life have moved on. Along the way I have learned the lessons that my decisions and experiences have given: the need for spirituality, patience, forgiveness, faith, flexibility, tenacity, buoyancy and to love unconditionally.

God has blessed me and kept me from crumbling completely by putting my broken pieces back together. Most of all, it is necessary for me to remember that regardless of my circumstances, He expects me to remain inwardly "sweet," until He returns for me.

Reminder:

A cookie is a cake made from stiff dough. No matter how crusty or hard the dough is on the outside, it is always sweet on the inside.

BIBLIOGRAPHY

Alcott, Louisa, *Little Women*. Boston: Roberts Brothers, 1868.

Hughes, Langston, *Tambourines to Glory*. New York: musical play produced by Harlem Moon Classics, 1956.

Rand, Ayn, *Atlas* Shrugged. New York: Random House, 1957.

Rand, Ayn, *The Fountainhead*. Indianapolis: Bobbs-Merrill, 1943.

Wolf, Thomas, *You Can't Go Home Again*, New York: Harper & Brothers, 1940. (posthumously)

Hellman, Lillian, *The Little Foxes*. New York: Publisher Viking Press, 1961.

Henley, Ernest, *Invictus,* The New Oxford Book of English Verse, Helen Gardner, Editor, Oxford University Press, U.S.A. (October 26, 1972)

Greensboro Daily News, *Dead Pastor's Friends Mourn "Leader of Men,* page 1, November 16, 1974.

The Whole Truth, *Three Thousand Pay Final Respects to Bishop Wells,* Volume VIII, NO. II, Memphis, Tennessee, February, 1975.

Private Dancer (CD Album), Part # 1108725, composers, *What's Love Got to Do with It*, Britten, Terry and Graham, Lyle, Catalog Number 55833

*Many, many years later, until his death, Joseph would ask my sister, Eva, about me.

*D.A., Bishop Dewitt Arthur Burton, was one of my dad's closest friend who visited daily. He died March 2013